MICKEY ROGERS
JOANNE TAYLORE-KNOWLES
STEVE TAYLORE-KNOWLES

SPEAK YOUR MIND

STUDENT'S BOOK
+ access to Student's App and Digital Workbook

2B

macmillan education

	Outcomes	Vocabulary	Grammar	Speaking
Unit 7 Get to Work pp. 67–75	• Talk about being career-ready • Discuss a successful person • Talk about skills and qualifications	• Career readiness • Success • Employability skills	• Present perfect with *already, yet,* and *just* • Present perfect and simple past Grammar Reference pp. 151–152	• Discuss how career-ready you are • Talk about someone with a nontraditional career • Discuss your creativity
	Language and Life—Problem-solving: Create a Business Plan for an Entrepreneur			
Unit 8 Downtime pp. 77–85	• Talk about kids' activities that adults like doing • Make plans and talk about preferences • Express your opinion	• Kidult activities • Leisure activities • Adjectives of feeling	• Gerund phrases as subject and object • Verb + gerund or infinitive Grammar Reference pp. 152–153	• Explain enjoyable kids' activities • Discuss weekend activities • Talk about doing nothing
	Language and Life—Mindfulness: Select Calming Activities to Relax Your Mind			
Unit 9 Room for Me pp. 87–95	• Talk about types of housing • Talk about living preferences • Discuss future changes in the home	• Housing solutions • Living together • Appliances	• Future forms • Future possibility and certainty Grammar Reference pp. 154–155	• Discuss housing • Talk about future possibilities • Talk about homes of the future
	Language and Life—Decision-making: Use a Decision Matrix to Plan and Develop a Neighborhood			
Unit 10 Wellbeing pp. 97–105	• Talk about study habits • Talk about hypothetical conditions • Write about small life changes	• Brain power • Accidents and illnesses • Collocations with *get*	• Zero and first conditional • Second conditional Grammar Reference pp. 155–156	• Express opinions about study habits • Role-play a conversation about illnesses • Discuss getting in shape and healthy
	Language and Life—Critical Thinking: Create Campaigns to Improve Public Health			
Unit 11 Use and Reuse pp. 107–115	• Talk about what things are made of • Talk about inventions and gifts • Discuss uses of plastic	• Product lifecycles • Clothing materials • Collocations connected to materials	• Simple present passive • Simple past passive Grammar Reference pp. 157–158	• Discuss the lifecycle of a plastic bottle • Talk about a gift you received • Compare how you use plastic
	Language and Life—Innovation: Suggest Upcycling Projects			
Unit 12 I'm a Member pp. 117–125	• Talk about social groups • Discuss networking • Talk about belonging to youth tribes	• Types of community • Networking • Appearance	• Reflexive pronouns • Review of tenses Grammar Reference pp. 158–159	• Discuss social groups • Talk about expanding your network • Discuss subcultures
	Language and Life—Media Literacy: Design an Ad Campaign to Reach a Target Group			

Confident Communicator	Pronunciation	Listening/Reading	Thinking Skills	Writing
Keep Talking • Give negative answers *Keep Talking* • Express doubt *Start Talking* • Describe images	• /j/ and /dʒ/	Read an informative article about career readiness • Skill—Understand vocabulary in context Listen to an interview with an entrepreneur • Skill—Understand attitude Listen to a lecture about employability skills • Skill—Identify key words	• Summarize • Analyze	Write a personal statement
Unit Review p. 76 **Study Skills** p. 133—Creativity				
Start Talking • Describe an activity *Keep Talking* • Agree with a proposal *Start Talking* • Explain a concept	• *–ould* words	Read an article about kidult activities • Skill—Read for main ideas Listen to people plan weekend activities • Skill—Listen for details Listen to a class discussion about the psychology of doing nothing • Skill—Listen for reasons	• Apply • Analyze • Understand	Write a blog entry
Unit Review p. 86 **Follow A Pro** p. 134—A Resort Activities Coordinator ▶ A Recreation Coordinator				
Keep Talking • Ask for opinions *Keep Talking* • Ask for reasons for opinions *Keep Talking* • Give reasons for opinions	• /aʊ/ and /oʊ/	Read an article about housing solutions • Skill—Predict Listen to a conversation about where to live • Skill—Listen for attitude Listen to a talk about solar panels • Skill—Take notes	• Understand • Evaluate	Write an opinion paragraph
Unit Review p. 96 **Study Skills** p. 135—Problem Solving				
Start Talking • State agreement or disagreement *Keep Talking* • Ask about an illness *Start Talking* • Make a statement stronger	• Intonation in conditional sentences	Read an article on ways to improve your memory • Skill—Scan Listen to an interview with a health expert • Skill—Listen for cause and effect Listen to a dialogue about a fitness program • Skill—Listen for gist	• Brainstorm • Evaluate • Understand	Write a website comment
Unit Review p. 106 **Follow A Pro** p. 136—A Family Physician ▶ A Physical Therapist				
Start Talking • Order steps in a process *Keep Talking* • State who made something *Start Talking* • State alternatives	• Silent *t*	Read an article about the lifecycle of a T-shirt • Skill—Understand words from context Listen to an interview about accidental discoveries • Skill—Listen for key words Listen to a lecture on upcycling items • Skill—Listen for gist	• Brainstorm • Understand • Analyze	Write an email
Unit Review p. 116 **Study Skills** p. 137—Using Precise Language in Academic Writing				
Start Talking • Make a guess *Start Talking* • Show certainty *Keep Talking* • Further a point	• /s/ vs. /ʃ/	Read an article on types of community • Skill—Understand the main ideas Listen to a podcast about networking • Skill—Listen for the main ideas Listen to an interview about different social groups • Skill—Listen for gist	• Analyze • Understand	Write a description
Unit Review p. 126 **Follow A Pro** p. 138—An Entrepreneur ▶ An Entrepreneur				

Grammar Quiz: What Do You Already Know?

A Complete the conversation with words from the box.

are   is   'm   not   's   's   what's

Esme: Hi, my name's Esme. **1** __________ your name?
Monique: My name **2** __________ Monique.
Esme: Nice to meet you, Monique. Where **3** __________ you from?
Monique: I **4** __________ from France. I work here. I'm an interpreter.
Esme: Really? That **5** __________ interesting.
Monique: It **6** __________. I love my job! What about you? Are you American?
Esme: No, I'm **7** __________. I'm British.

B Complete the paragraph with the simple present form of the verbs in parentheses.

My sister, Emily, really **1** __________ (love) her phone. She **2** __________ (check) her phone when she **3** __________ (wake) up. I think she **4** __________ (send) about a hundred text messages a day! She **5** __________ (use) about five different social media sites, too. I **6** __________ (have) a smartphone, too, but I can live without it. I **7** __________ (not need) to post pictures of my food every time I have a nice meal! What about you? How much time **8** __________ you __________ (spend) on your phone?

C Choose the correct option.

Leo: What **1 do you have** / **are you having** for lunch today, Jill?
Jill: Today **2 I'm having** / **I have** noodle salad with shrimp and chili sauce.
Leo: It looks delicious! **3 Did you buy** / **Do you bought** it from the café?
Jill: No, **4 I made it** / **I'm making it** at home. It's cheap, and it's healthy, too.
Leo: I think I **5 should** / **could** start to bring food from home. The cafeteria always **6 serves** / **serving** the same things. I **7 want to** / **want** eat a more balanced diet.

D Find one error in each line of the conversation. Write the corrected sentence.

Rob: Is you almost ready, Julie? **1** __________
Julie: Yes! I'm so excited about going to the Amsterdam! **2** __________
Rob: Where do you want to do when we're there? **3** __________
Julie: I want to go sightseeing around a city. **4** __________
Rob: Yeah, I like to do that, too. Can we go by bicycle? **5** __________
Julie: I'd like to, but I can ride a bike! **6** __________

E Complete the email with words from the box.

a   a   her   's   the   the   X (no article)   your

Hi Malu,

Thanks for your email! I'm really excited about **1** __________ school trip to France next summer. **2** __________ hometown looks beautiful. It's great that there is **3** __________ waterfall just three kilometers away. Is there **4** __________ forest, too? I love **5** __________ trees! Can we climb **6** __________ mountain you told me about? I know the weather is sometimes rainy in France, so I've borrowed my friend **7** __________ waterproof jacket and I've also borrowed **8** __________ walking boots.

See you soon!

Reba

Go to the Grammar Review on pages 140–141

UNIT 7

Get to Work

WHAT DO YOU ALREADY KNOW?

1 **Think about the career you want and the qualifications and abilities you need to be successful. Write the words.**

2 **IN PAIRS** **Share and compare your ideas. Add more words to your lists.**

Qualifications

Abilities

VIDEO

DISCUSS & SHARE

3 **IN GROUPS** **Watch the video and answer the question.**

SYM Are you born with talent or is it something you learn?

In this unit, you will ...

- talk about career readiness, career alternatives, and employability skills.
- use thinking skills: summarize and analyze.
- read about being ready for a career.
- use strategies to start and keep talking by giving negative answers, expressing doubt, and describing images.
- use problem-solving skills to create a business plan for an entrepreneur.
- learn tips for developing creativity.

LESSON 1 Are You Career-Ready?

READING

A **What is the difference between a career and a job? Discuss as a class.**

B **7.01 IN PAIRS THINKING SKILL—Summarize Read the article. Together, describe in your own words the three main factors in being career-ready.**

How Career-Ready Are You?

Have you started your career yet? If you have just started working, you are probably very happy and are learning a lot about your job. However, if you have already worked for a while, you are probably thinking about how to **improve** your career options. If you haven't started working yet, you are probably thinking about what kind of career you want. It is always a good idea to think about the next step in your working life.

First, it is important to understand that being **career-ready** refers to more than training and knowledge about a job or a career. It refers to a combination of **knowledge**, skills, and personal characteristics.

Knowledge includes the academic or technical information that you need for a career area or a specific job, but it also includes other types of knowledge. For example, you may need general math skills or a good level of English.

Skills include specific technical skills, but they also include skills like using your time well, the **ability** to communicate, and working in a team. One of the most important skills today is the ability to **solve** problems.

Finally, you need to understand what personal characteristics and personality types are ideal for different jobs and careers. Some people with excellent academic **qualifications** are unhappy in their careers because their jobs don't really match their personalities.

It doesn't matter if you have just graduated from high school or college, haven't graduated yet, or already have a job; you should take some time to think about your future. How career-ready are you?

C **READING SKILL—Understand vocabulary in context Choose the meaning of the words in bold from the article in B.**

1 improve
a make something better **b** understand **c** know about

2 career-ready
a prepared to work **b** ready to go to college **c** having skills for a specific job

3 knowledge
a only academic information **b** the opposite of *opinion* **c** the facts you know about a topic

4 ability
a a fact **b** a skill **c** a characteristic

5 solve
a find a solution or an answer **b** understand **c** think about

6 qualifications
a grades in school **b** skills or experience you need for a job **c** hobbies

VOCABULARY

A **Complete the sentences with words from the box.**

career	degree	knowledge	qualifications	skill	training

1 Many companies have ______________ programs to teach their employees new technology.
2 The ability to work well with other people is an important ______________.
3 For many jobs, you have to have a college ______________.
4 Primary school teachers have to have a lot of ______________ about many subjects.
5 Good math and technical skills are ______________ for engineering jobs.
6 For a successful ______________, you need a combination of knowledge and skills.

GRAMMAR present perfect with *already, yet,* and *just*

A Read the first paragraph of the article in READING B and underline sentences with *already*, *just*, and *yet*.

B Complete the grammar rules with *already*, *just*, and *yet*.

1. To indicate that an action happened in the very recent past, use ____________ and the present perfect.
2. To indicate that an action has happened, sometimes sooner than expected, use ____________ and the present perfect.
3. To indicate that an action is going to happen but hasn't happened, use ____________ and the negative present perfect.
4. To ask if an action has happened, use ____________ and the present perfect in a question.

For more practice, go to page 151.

C Complete the conversations with *already*, *just*, and *yet*.

1. A: Have you studied for your test ____________? B: Yes, I've ____________ finished studying.
2. A: I haven't read the story for English class ____________. B: I've ____________ read it. It was good.
3. A: Has my package arrived ____________? B: I don't know. Oh, here it is. It has ____________ arrived.
4. A: It's only six o'clock and I've ____________ finished my homework. B: Really? I haven't started mine ____________!

D In your notebook, write something that you have already done today, something you have just done in the last few minutes, and something you haven't done yet today.

E IN PAIRS Ask and answer questions that you wrote in D.

PRONUNCIATION /j/ and /dʒ/

A 7.02 Listen and say the words. Pay attention to the sound of the first letter. Then answer: In which sound is your tongue closer to your top teeth?

yard	year	yellow	yes	yesterday	yet	you	young
jacket	jet	job	John	juice	Julie	jump	just

B 7.03 IN PAIRS Listen and repeat. Then practice reading together. Correct each other's pronunciation when necessary.

1. Julie bought a yellow jacket yesterday.
2. Yes, you can have some juice.
3. Have you met John yet?
4. James has just started a new job in New York.

SPEAKING

A IN PAIRS Make a list in your notebook of any skills, abilities, training, and qualifications you have. Do you think you're career-ready?

B IN GROUPS Discuss your lists and decide who you think is the most career-ready. Use the Confident Communicator box to help you.

CONFIDENT COMMUNICATOR
KEEP TALKING

When we give negative answers, we often add reasons or further information.

A: *Have you graduated yet?*
B: *Not yet. / No, I haven't. / No, but I'm going to graduate this year.*

A: *What have you done to improve your knowledge in social work?*
B: *Nothing (yet). / I haven't done anything (yet), but I'm going to do an internship*

Career Alternatives

LISTENING

A Discuss the questions as a class.

1 Do you need a business degree to have your own business?
2 In general, do you need a college degree to have a successful career?

B 7.04 Listen to the interview. Choose *True* or *False*.

1	Carmen's business sells food.	True / False
2	The business was very small when she started it.	True / False
3	Carmen studied business in college.	True / False
4	She graduated from college.	True / False
5	She started making ice cream as a hobby.	True / False
6	Customers like the flavor that Carmen has just created.	True / False

C 7.04 LISTENING SKILL—Understand attitude Listen again. Write the words from the box that indicate the speakers' attitudes.

bored excellent fantastic great not interested

1 Carmen's opinion of the ice cream: ______________
2 The interviewer's opinion of the ice cream: ______________
3 How Carmen felt one summer: ______________
4 Carmen's attitude toward college: ______________
5 Carmen's opinion of her sister's idea: ______________

D THINKING SKILL—Analyze Compare how Carmen felt about learning about ice cream to how she felt about learning about architecture. How does motivation help you succeed?

VOCABULARY success

A Complete the text with words from the box.

apply for a job	career path	get a promotion	hires
benefits	get a degree	get a raise	the corporate ladder

The key to success has traditionally been fairly similar for most people. You **1** ______________ and then you **2** ______________. If you're lucky, a good company **3** ______________ you, and you get a good salary and **4** ______________. After working for a while, you **5** ______________, and you usually also **6** ______________ in your salary. If you are good at your job, you climb **7** ______________. However, these days many people do not follow the traditional **8** ______________. Many young people are choosing to be entrepreneurs and start their own businesses. Most do this after college, but some don't graduate or don't go to college at all. There are many different ways to have a successful career.

B IN PAIRS Number the list in order of importance to you. Then share your list. Add more things, if possible.

_____ a good salary

_____ the chance to learn new things

_____ the chance to get frequent raises

_____ good benefits like a company car, health insurance, or long vacations

_____ the chance to get promotions and climb the corporate ladder

GRAMMAR present perfect and simple past

A Match the examples from the interview (1–8) to the descriptions (a–h). Write the letter.

1 We've been in business for five years now. _____
2 When school was out in the spring, I opened the ice cream shop. _____
3 I made the ice cream and she served the customers. _____
4 I made about 20 kinds of ice cream that summer. _____
5 How many flavors have you invented so far? _____
6 I've just created a new flavor called Orange Chill. _____
7 Have you started selling it yet? _____
8 We've already sold out! _____

a an event that happened at a specific time in the past
b an event that happened sooner than expected
c routines in the past
d an event that happened at the same time or immediately after another event
e a question about whether something has happened
f an action that has been in progress for an amount of time
g an action that happened in the very recent past
h an action that began in the past and will continue in the future

For more practice, go to page 152.

B Complete the text with the present perfect or simple past forms of the verbs in parentheses.

Carmen Vega's ice cream shop **1** ______________ (be) open for about five years. Carmen **2** ______________ (take) a class to learn how to make ice cream, and since then she **3** ______________ (invent) a lot of new ice cream flavors. When her shop **4** ______________ (open), only Carmen and one other person **5** ______________ (work) there, but in the past four years, she **6** ______________ (hire) 10 more people. She **7** ______________ (not open) any more shops yet, but she wants to open two more next year. It **8** ______________ (be) a great success so far!

MAKE IT REAL

In American English, people often use the simple past instead of the present perfect:
Did you eat yet? = Have you eaten yet?
I just bought a car. = I've just bought a car.
I already did my homework. = I've already done my homework.

SPEAKING

A Make notes about a person you know about who has been successful with a non-traditional career path.

- Who is the person and what did he/she do?
- Did that person go to college?
- How did the person prepare for his/her career?
- What else has the person done?

B IN GROUPS Discuss the career of the person you chose in A. Use the Confident Communicator box to help you.

CONFIDENT COMMUNICATOR
KEEP TALKING

Use these phrases to express doubt or uncertainty when you answer a question:
Yes/No questions: *I (don't) think so. / Maybe. I don't (really) know. / I'm not sure.*
Information questions: *I'm not sure. / I don't (really) know.*

VOCABULARY employability skills

A Complete the sentences with words from the box.

creative curious flexible honest independent motivated organized

1 If you can make changes when necessary, you are ______________.
2 Paul is very ______________. He always plans and does things in a logical order.
3 Sandra enjoys working alone. She's very ______________.
4 If you always tell the truth, you are ______________.
5 Martina works hard and is very ______________. She wants to get a promotion.
6 If you have a lot of new, interesting ideas, you are ______________.
7 Most children are very ______________ and like learning about many things.

B Write the words from A in the appropriate categories.

Types of employability skills		
Intrapersonal (personal characteristics)	Interpersonal (how you interact with people)	Cognitive (thinking skills)

LISTENING

A 7.05 You are going to listen to a talk called *Getting a Job in the 21st Century*. What do you think the main idea of the talk will be? Listen and check your answer.

B 7.05 LISTENING SKILL—Identify key words Listen again. Choose all of the things the speakers mentioned.

1 In the past, employers usually focused on … and …
a a high school diploma b a college degree c personality d work experience
2 Someone who is …, …, and … could get a better job than someone with a degree.
a organized b creative c interesting d motivated
3 In the example, James got the job because he was …, …, and …
a friendly b flexible c curious d motivated
4 The speaker says that it's best to have … and …
a a college degree b excellent skills c good contacts d great qualifications

MAKE IT YOURS

Think of characteristics and skills that are important in your career area. Make a list and share it with classmates in the same career area.

WRITING

A **Read the personal statement. Then choose *True* or *False*.**

> ### PERSONAL STATEMENT
>
> I am an English teacher, and I have taught at a language school in Sao Paulo for five years. I have a degree in education from the University of Virginia, but I'm Brazilian, so I know that it's very difficult to learn English! I'm very patient, and I'm good at communicating with my students. I enjoy working with my students and my colleagues. I'm very motivated, and I have just taken some extra courses in classroom management and teaching techniques. I think one of my best qualities is curiosity because teachers should always want to learn new things.

1 A personal statement has information about things like family and pets. True / False
2 The statement gives some information about education and work experience. True / False
3 The statement has a complete list of degrees and work experience. True / False
4 The statement has some information about the writer's personality. True / False
5 The statement is a general introduction to the writer. True / False

B **Make general notes about your skills and qualifications in your notebook. Then use your notes to write a personal statement.**

C **IN PAIRS Read each other's personal statements. Circle any incorrect verb forms. Make suggestions for adding information.**

> **MAKE IT DIGITAL**
>
> When you get ready to write a resume, look up sample resumes and personal statements online. Find one that is appropriate for you and use it as a model.

SPEAKING

A **Many employers say they want employees who are creative. Use basic geometric shapes to create a drawing on a piece of paper. It doesn't matter if you have artistic talent or not. The objective is to think creatively!**

square circle rectangle triangle oval

B **IN GROUPS Compare your drawings. If necessary, explain your drawing. Use the Confident Communicator box to help you. In your opinion, who has the most creative drawing?**

> **CONFIDENT COMMUNICATOR**
> **START TALKING**
>
> Describing geometric images:
> *I've used five circles to create a …*
> *I've put together eight triangles to represent a …*
> *The oval shape is a …*
> *The rectangle and the square form a …*

Language and Life

Problem-solving – Becoming an Entrepreneur

A 7.06 **Read the article. Then discuss the questions as a class.**

1 What is the main characteristic of all of the business possibilities in the article?
2 What specific characteristics and skills are mentioned in the article?
3 What is one of the easiest businesses to start and run? Why?

Turn Skills into Sales

Have you ever thought about starting your own business? These days, more and more young people are doing just that. There are many types of businesses that are not very expensive to start. Often you just need a computer, but you also need to be motivated and patient because starting a business takes a lot of time and hard work.

There are several areas that offer good business opportunities for young people.

- If you are creative, make handmade items: clothes, jewelry, soap, hand-painted T-shirts, origami designs, or greeting cards.

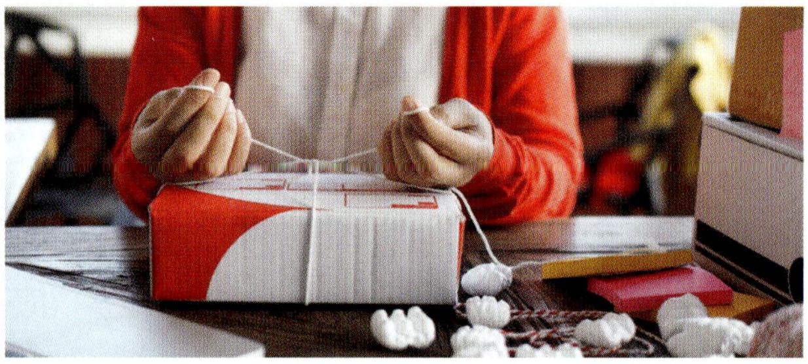

- Are you good at photography? Take pictures and sell them to online stock photo companies. Take photos or make videos of events like weddings, family reunions, or community events. Start a pet portrait business.
- Can you cook? Make cookies or cupcakes to sell to friends, at community events, or online.
- Do you love animals? Think about dog walking or pet sitting. You can also make different flavors of dog treats.
- If you have good computer skills, there are many possibilities for making money. Start a device setup service to help people get started with new computers, tablets, phones, or any other device. Become a tech tutor to teach children or older people how to use computers.
- Do you like public speaking, writing, or performing? If you have interesting things to say, you can start a blog or a vlog and get money from advertisers. Maybe you can become a video personality, or create videos to teach people how to do things.
- Finally, one of the easiest ways to make money is to sell things online. Sell items that your family doesn't use anymore, and buy things online or at garage sales and resell them.

B IN PAIRS **Write three possible small business ideas in the table. Check the criteria that apply to each business.**

Business idea	We have experience in this work.	We know a lot about this.	It isn't too expensive to start.	It's fun.	We don't need a store or an office.
1	☐	☐	☐	☐	☐
2	☐	☐	☐	☐	☐
3	☐	☐	☐	☐	☐

C IN PAIRS **For each business you chose in B, make a list of education, experience, skills, and personality characteristics that you think are necessary for that business.**

Business 1
Education: ______
Experience: ______
Knowledge or skills: ______
Personality characteristics: ______

Business 2
Education: ______
Experience: ______
Knowledge or skills: ______
Personality characteristics: ______

Business 3
Education: ______
Experience: ______
Knowledge or skills: ______
Personality characteristics: ______

D IN PAIRS **Choose the business that you think would be the best for you and your partner. Consider your experience and personality characteristics. Complete the business profile.**

SMALL BUSINESS PROFILE

Type of business: ______
Name of business: ______
Location (online, store, etc.): ______
Products or services: ______
Main customers: ______

E IN GROUPS **Present your business idea. Vote on the best business idea.**

F **Discuss the questions.**

1 What was the most important part of your decision?
2 In what other situations do you use problem-solving skills to make decisions?

MAKE IT DIGITAL

Do research online about small business opportunities in your country or your area. Share the ideas with your class

VOCABULARY review

SCORE: / 10

A Complete the sentences with words from the box.

apply benefits career curious degree flexible hired motivated raises skills

I have a **1** ____________ from a good university, and now I'm ready to start my **2** ____________. I want to be a nurse, and I think I have the **3** ____________ to get **4** ____________ at a good hospital. I'm **5** ____________ to work hard, and I'm very **6** ____________ about medical information. I like to learn new things. I'm also very **7** ____________ with my working hours. I'm going to **8** ____________ for a job at two hospitals in my city. I would prefer Central Hospital because they have good **9** ____________, like health insurance, and they give **10** ____________ if you do a good job.

GRAMMAR review

SCORE: / 10

A Complete the sentences with the correct forms of the verbs in parentheses.

I'm really excited because I **1** ____________ just ____________ (start) my own business! I **2** ____________ (be) very busy my first week. I **3** ____________ already ____________ (send) about 100 emails to friends, and yesterday I **4** ____________ (put) my new website online. I **5** ____________ (not have) many orders yet, but I'm not worried!

B Unscramble and write sentences.

1 I / my / business online / started / new / just / have / .

____

2 interview / a / gotten / he / yet / hasn't / job / .

____

3 written / you / your / have / yet / resume / ?

____

4 already / my / I've / resume / finished / .

____

5 check / yesterday / I / listings / didn't / job / .

____

16–20 correct: You can talk about success and employability skills. You can use the present perfect with *already*, *yet*, and *just*.
0–15 correct: Look again at the Vocabulary and Grammar sections in the unit.

TOTAL SCORE: / 20

WHAT DO YOU KNOW NOW? Look back at page 67 and add the words you know now to the boxes.

STUDY SKILLS CREATIVITY

A Take the quiz. Then go to **Study Skills** on page 133. Find the answers and learn more about creativity.

1 **... of people have creative ideas in the shower.**
a 59% **b** 69% **c** 72%

2 **Aerobic exercise makes you less creative.**
a True **b** False

3 **...of people think they could be more creative.**
a 50% **b** 75% **c** 98%

4 **... of CEOs think that creativity is the most important quality for leaders to have.**
a 35% **b** 60% **c** 90%

UNIT 8

Downtime

WHAT DO YOU ALREADY KNOW?

1 **Read the definition of *downtime*. Then think of different types of activities you do when you have downtime.**

downtime (n.): a time when you are not working or busy

2 **Compare and share your activities. Add more words to your lists.**

Relaxing activities

Energetic activities

VIDEO

DISCUSS & SHARE

3 **IN GROUPS** **Watch the video and answer the question.**

SYM Do you have a lot of downtime, or are you always busy?

In this unit, you will ...

- talk about creative activities for adults, leisure activities for a weekend, and "do nothing" time.
- use thinking skills: apply, analyze, and understand.
- read about "kidults."
- use strategies to repair talking by describing an activity, agreeing with a proposal, and explaining a concept.
- use mindfulness to manage your life and relax your mind.
- follow a resort activities coordinator to learn about this job and the skills needed for the leisure industry.

VOCABULARY

A Label the pictures with the activities from the box.

building a model	coloring	flying a kite	making things with clay

1 

____

2 

____

3 

____

4 

____

MAKE IT YOURS

Find the names of three or more activities that you liked doing when you were a child. Do you still like doing them?

READING

A As a class, discuss what you think the term *kidult* refers to.

B 8.01 READING SKILL— Read for main ideas Read the text. Then match the main ideas (1–4) to the paragraphs (a–d). Write the letter.

KIDS + ADULTS = KIDULTS

a Adults like having toys—no, not boats, sports equipment, or expensive audio equipment, but actual children's toys. They are making things with building blocks, coloring in coloring books, making art with 3D pens, and doing difficult puzzles; they are bouncing inside enormous plastic balls and flying kites. There is a new term for adults who love playing like children: *kidults*.

b Why is this happening? Experts think that in part it is because people, especially millennials, want an escape from the complications of the modern world. Acting like a child is a way to return to a simpler time, but there is another reason for this trend. Doing kids' activities is fun! Why shouldn't adults enjoy doing things like flying kites or coloring?

c People over 50 also spend time doing children's activities. Many grandparents are very healthy and active, and they love playing with their grandchildren. Seniors are playing board games, doing arts and crafts, and participating in other activities that kids love.

d Being an adult doesn't mean that you have to be serious all the time or pay a lot of money for entertainment. Are you creative? Try building a model or making a sculpture with clay. Maybe you love being active, but you can't stand playing competitive sports. Try jumping rope or flying a kite. Find your inner child and enjoy being a kidult!

1 There are two main reasons why young people like being kidults. Paragraph ____

2 Adults are doing many children's activities. Paragraph ____

3 You don't always have to act like an adult. Paragraph ____

4 There is a large group of older *kidults*. Paragraph ____

C **IN PAIRS** **Discuss the questions. Look back at the text in B for help if necessary.**

1 According to the article, what is the definition of *kidults*?
2 What are the two main reasons that adults like being kidults?
3 According to the article, kidult activities are not necessarily expensive. Which ideas in the article are inexpensive? Which are probably a little expensive?

D **THINKING SKILL—Apply** **Think about things you like to do in your leisure time. Do you think you are or could be a kidult? Why or why not?**

GRAMMAR gerund phrases as subject and object

A **Read the sentences and answer the questions.**

a Acting like a child is a way to return to a simpler time.
b People over 50 also often prefer doing children's activities.

1 What is the subject in sentence *a*? ______________________
2 What is the object in sentence *b*? ______________________
3 What is similar between the subject in *a* and the object in *b*? ______________________
4 What form of the verb is used after *prefer, enjoy, can't stand, like, love,* and *hate*? ______________________

For more practice, go to page 153.

B **Look back at READING B. Underline two more examples of gerunds as subjects and two more examples of gerunds as objects.**

C **Write answers for you using gerunds.**

1 Are there any children's toys that you enjoy playing with?
I enjoy making model cars.
2 How can playing with children be good for older people?
____
3 Do you think being a kidult is a good idea for young adults? Why or why not?
____

D **IN PAIRS** **Discuss your ideas from C.**

SPEAKING

A **Make a list of kids' activities that you enjoy or would enjoy doing.**

B **IN GROUPS** **Tell your group the activities you chose and explain why. If necessary, explain what an activity is. Use the Confident Communicator box to help you.**

A: I love playing Hide-and-Seek. It's great because you play with friends, you get exercise, and you laugh a lot.
B: What's Hide-and-Seek?
A: You play in a group. One person is "It." The others hide and the person has to try to find them ....

CONFIDENT COMMUNICATOR
START TALKING

You can use these phrases to describe an activity or a game:
You play … on teams / in a group / on a field.
There's … a base / a large ball.
One person is … "It" / the leader.
You have to … bounce a ball / run to a base / find the person.

Plan for Fun!

VOCABULARY leisure activities

A Match the words from the box to the verbs (1–4). Use a dictionary if necessary.

a barbecue	aerobics	jewelry	paddle boarding	to a park
a potluck meal	furniture	kayaking	skating	yoga

Leisure activities

1 Have: a picnic, ______________, ______________
2 Make: pottery, ______________, ______________
3 Do: crafts, ______________, ______________
4 Go: for a drive, ______________, ______________, ______________, ______________

B Complete the online comments with the correct forms of *have*, *make*, *do*, and *go*.

I do all kinds of things that people say help with stress. I **1** ______________ yoga; in fact, I **2** ______________ to my yoga class four days a week. I almost always **3** ______________ swimming or skating on weekends, and I also **4** ______________ aerobics. I exercise a lot, but I'm still really stressed! Molly

@Molly Wow, you need to relax! **5** ______________ yoga and lots of exercise is great, but what about relaxing and having fun? **6** ______________ a craft—**7** ______________ jewelry or candles, or color in a coloring book. I **8** ______________ really bad furniture, but it's fun and relaxing! Jen

@Jen I'm not into arts and crafts, but I agree with Jen. Relax! I like **9** ______________ for a drive in the country or **10** ______________ a picnic with friends. Get together with a group of friends and **11** ______________ a potluck meal or **12** ______________ to a park. Have some fun! Lance

LISTENING

A Take a class survey and answer the questions.

1 How many people usually do more or less the same activities every weekend?
2 What are some of the most common weekend activities?
3 How many people usually plan their weekend activities ahead of time?

B 8.02 LISTENING SKILL—Listen for details Listen to a conversation about weekend activities. Answer the questions. Listen again to check.

1 What activities does Kate describe as "the same stuff"?
2 What does Ken say he does not like doing?
3 What activities do they decide to do on Saturday?
4 What do they decide to do on Sunday?

C THINKING SKILL—Analyze Write the activities from the conversation in B in the categories below. Add other activities to each category.

1 Creative: ______________
2 Cultural: going to a movie, ______________
3 Physical: ______________
4 Social: hanging out at somebody's house, ______________

GRAMMAR verb + gerund or infinitive

A Read the sentences. Then choose the correct form of the verb to complete the rules. Choose more than one option if possible.

I love going out to hear live music.
I like to go to dinner and a movie.
I prefer to watch TV at home.
I prefer doing physical activities.
I'd like to do something creative.
I'd rather do a physical activity.
I would prefer to have the picnic first.

1 *love, like, hate, prefer* + base verb / infinitive / *–ing* verb
2 *would like* + base verb / infinitive / *–ing* verb
3 *would prefer* + base verb / infinitive / *–ing* verb
4 *would rather* + base verb / infinitive / *–ing* verb

For more practice, go to page 154.

B Complete the email with the correct form of the verbs in parentheses.

Hey, guys. Would you like **1** ____________ (see) the boat show this weekend? I can get tickets for either Saturday or Sunday. I'd rather **2** ____________ (go) on Sunday, I think, because I prefer **3** ____________ (do) housework and errands on Saturdays. Also, I'd rather **4** ____________ (take) the bus because I hate **5** ____________ (drive) in a lot of traffic, and I'd kind of prefer **6** ____________ (get) there early. What do you think? Does all of that sound OK?

PRONUNCIATION *–ould* words

A 8.03 Listen to the conversation and answer the questions.

Omar: Would you like to go to the new museum tomorrow?
Jamal: That sounds great. We should go early, when there are fewer people.
Omar: Actually, I would rather go in the afternoon. Is that OK?
Jamal: That's fine. Could you pick me up?
Omar: Sure.

1 Do *would*, *should*, and *could* have the same vowel sound or different sounds?
2 Do you hear the *l* in *would*, *should*, and *could*?

B IN PAIRS Practice the conversation. Pay special attention to the pronunciation of *would*, *should*, and *could*.

MAKE IT REAL

Although the meaning of *hate*, *like*, *love*, and *prefer* is the same when used with an infinitive or with a gerund, the infinitive form is more commonly used in American English than the gerund form.

SPEAKING

A IN PAIRS In your notebook, make a list of activities that you can do in your area in each category.

- Creative
- Cultural
- Physical
- Social

B IN GROUPS Compare your lists from A. Create one list of activities that you all like doing.

C IN GROUPS Discuss activities for a group activity weekend. Use the Confident Communicator box to help you.

A: I love / like / don't really like / can't stand …
B: I would like to / prefer to / rather …

CONFIDENT COMMUNICATOR
KEEP TALKING

Agreeing with a proposal
Sure. / That's fine with me. / That sounds good.

Objecting to a proposal
The problem is that … / Sorry, but I don't really like … / Unfortunately, I can't …

LESSON 3 Is It OK to Do Nothing?

LISTENING

A **Do you enjoy doing nothing? Why or why not? Discuss as a class.**

B **8.04 LISTENING SKILL—Listen for reasons Listen to a class discussion and check (✓) the reasons you hear for and against doing nothing.**

For
- ☐ It's fun.
- ☐ It helps you relax.
- ☐ It helps you be more creative.
- ☐ It helps you solve problems.

Against
- ☐ It's boring.
- ☐ It makes you tired.
- ☐ It makes you feel guilty.
- ☐ It's unhealthy.

C **THINKING SKILL—Understand List the examples of activities that are classified as *doing nothing* in the class discussion from B. Add several more examples of activities that you consider to be *doing nothing*.**

____

____

____

____

VOCABULARY adjectives of feeling

A **Match the words from the box to the definitions (1–5).**

bored	guilty	nervous	rested	stressed

1. ______________: worried or a little scared
2. ______________: not interested in the activity or conversation
3. ______________: feeling bad because you are doing something wrong
4. ______________: worried about professional, financial, or personal problems
5. ______________: not tired

B **IN PAIRS Ask and answer the questions.**

1. How do you feel when you do nothing?
2. What situations make you feel nervous?
3. What do you do if you feel stressed?
4. When do you get bored?

A: I feel bored when I do nothing.

B: I eat when I feel stressed.

WRITING

A Read the blog entry. Then answer the questions.

MY PROFILE

Some people say that it's good to do nothing, but I disagree. I think doing nothing is bad for you. First, most people think that doing nothing is not productive, and I agree. It's better to use your time studying, working, or helping other people. Second, some people say that doing nothing helps you think creatively and solve problems. However, when people say they are doing nothing, they are usually doing things like looking at social media or watching TV. Those activities don't help you think creatively or solve problems. Finally, the main problem is that doing nothing can become a habit. If you take a break to relax and do nothing, it is difficult to start working or studying again. It is easier if you finish working or studying before you take a break.

1. How many reasons does the writer give to support his argument? ______
2. What words does the writer use to indicate that he is introducing a new point? ______
3. Where does the writer place his most important argument? ______

B In your opinion, is it good or bad to do nothing? Think about the question and make notes in your notebook.

C Use your notes from B to write a blog entry in your notebook.

D IN PAIRS Exchange papers with someone who has the opposite opinion from yours. Read each other's blog entries and then discuss the question.

Did your partner's arguments change your opinion?

SPEAKING

A Make notes on the questions.

1. How often do you do nothing?

______

______

2. When you do nothing, what do you do?

______

______

B IN GROUPS Compare your ideas. Say what the perfect do-nothing day would be for you. Use the Confident Communicator box to help you.

A: On a do-nothing day, I'd like to … *B: Really? I'd rather …*

CONFIDENT COMMUNICATOR
START TALKING

Explaining a concept
Doing nothing **means** *sitting around just thinking about things.*
To me, *doing nothing* **is** *reading a good book and not going out.*
For me, *the perfect do-nothing day is sitting/going/having …*
I think *doing nothing* **is when** *you …*

Language and Life

Mindfulness – Relaxing Your Mind

A 8.05 IN PAIRS Read the article. Then discuss the questions.

MINDFULNESS FOR MENTAL RELAXATION

Study, work, family, friends, pets, social media ... We feel tired and stressed because we can't do everything. The effects of this are that we are less efficient, less creative, and less happy. We all try to do leisure activities like playing sports or watching movies, but what about leisure time for the mind?

In recent years, many people have started to practice *mindfulness*. Being mindful means that you are paying attention to what you are doing at the moment, to your feelings, and to the things that are happening around you. You are not thinking about things that have already happened or worrying about what is going to happen. For example, if you notice how the sun feels on your face, or how your clean clothes smell, you are being mindful.

There are some simple things that you can do to practice mindfulness. Do you like walking? Go for a walk, but don't think about walking fast or going a certain distance. Walk slowly. Think about how your body feels. Stop and look at trees or flowers. Stop and close your eyes. What do you hear, feel, or smell? Would you rather do something creative? Paint something or do a craft. Don't worry if it isn't good. Think about the process. How does the paintbrush feel in your hand? What does each color make you think of? Giving your brain time to relax can help you feel less stressed and more rested. The result is more creativity and better problem solving.

1 What are the effects of being tired and stressed?
2 What is mindfulness?
3 How is a mindful activity different from the normal way we do things?
4 What are the effects of giving your brain time to relax?

B Choose one of the mindfulness activities and try it.

Positive reflection (5 minutes)

1. Think of three things that you are thankful for and write them down.
2. Think of three good things that you have done or that have happened to you this week and write them down.
3. Close your eyes. Breathe slowly. Take a few minutes to reflect on the things on your lists. How do you feel?

Observation (5 minutes)

1. Go to a window in your classroom. If there are no windows, choose an area of your classroom to focus on.
2. Look at everything you see. Don't think about the names of the things at all. Notice shapes and colors.
3. Notice changes in the light or movement of the objects.
4. If you start thinking about other things, notice a color or a shape again. Focus only on that color or shape.

Visualization (5 minutes)

1. Think of a place that you love. Close your eyes and imagine that you are in that place.
2. Think about what is around you. For example, if you are in the mountains, what do you see? Are there tall trees? Is there snow on the mountains? Is the grass green?
3. Use your other senses. What do you smell? Flowers? What do you hear? Birds singing? A waterfall? What do you feel? The sun? A cool wind on your skin?
4. Breathe slowly and relax. If you start thinking about other things, focus on the details of the place.

C IN GROUPS Discuss your experience. Use the questions as a guide.

1. Which activity did you choose?
2. Was it easy or hard to do the activity?
3. How do you feel after the activity?
4. Did you like doing the activity?
5. Do you think mindfulness activities can help your mind relax when you are feeling stressed?

D IN PAIRS Choose a situation and suggest a mindfulness activity to help the person feel less stressed. You can use an activity from B or invent your own activity.

1. Paul is very nervous about a big exam tomorrow. He's at home, and he's trying to study, but he can't concentrate. He's messaging friends on social media and saying that he thinks the exam will be very hard.
2. Sam is worried about his health. He knows that he doesn't always eat well and he doesn't sleep enough. When he worries, he eats junk food and watches TV very late at night. He says that junk food and action movies make him feel happy!
3. Kathy is on the bus, on her way to her university classes. There is a lot of traffic, and the bus is going very slowly. Kathy is really bored, and she is getting angry because she's probably going to be late for class.

E IN GROUPS Share your mindfulness activity from D with your group. Then discuss the questions.

1. Have you ever been in any of the situations in **D**? How did you feel? What did you do?
2. Of the ideas that you heard, which activities would you prefer to do?

F Discuss the questions.

1. Was it useful to take time to relax? Why or why not?
2. What other ways do you use to calm yourself?

MAKE IT DIGITAL

Do research to find more mindfulness activities. Choose one or two and try them. Use questions 1–5 from **C** to report to your class about the activities you did.

VOCABULARY review

SCORE: / 10

A Complete the sentences with the words in the box.

kite	coloring	potluck	crafts	model	skating

1 We're going to have a big ____________ meal. Everyone is going to bring a different dish.
2 My dad's hobby is building ____________ airplanes.
3 It's windy today – a great day for flying a ____________.
4 It's a nice day. Let's go ____________ in the park.
5 I do a lot of different ____________. It's relaxing and creative.
6 I love ____________ pictures. I usually use colored pencils.

B Choose the correct option.

1 I'm worried about work because I have too much to do. I'm really **bored / guilty / stressed**.
2 I'm not doing anything, and my friends are all busy. I'm **bored / stressed / rested**.
3 I had a great weekend. I saw friends and slept a lot. I feel very **guilty / bored / rested**.
4 My brother didn't invite his friend Joe to the party. Now he feels **stressed / guilty / nervous**.

GRAMMAR review

SCORE: / 10

A Complete the email with the correct form of the verbs in parentheses.

Hey, Susie. You love **1** ____________ (do) crafts, right? I'm taking a cool art class. We're learning to create art with different materials. I don't like **2** ____________ (paint) or **3** ____________ (draw), but **4** ____________ (make) models or clay sculptures is really fun! Also, we're, **5** ____________ (make) cool jewelry out of paper. Would you like **6** ____________ (go) to a class with me? Is Monday OK, or would you prefer **7** ____________ (go) on Wednesday? I'd rather **8** ____________ (take) you on Monday if possible. I think you'll like **9** ____________ (visit) the class, and I'm sure you'd rather **10** ____________ (go) to an art class than study for the math exam. 🙂

16–20 correct: You can discuss leisure activities and use adjectives of feeling. You can use gerunds.
0–15 correct: Look again at the Vocabulary and Grammar sections in the unit.

TOTAL SCORE: / 20

WHAT DO YOU KNOW NOW? Look back at page 77 and add the words you know now to the boxes.

FOLLOW A PRO LEISURE

Take the quiz about activities coordinators. Then go to **Follow A Pro** on page 134. Find the answers and learn more about the leisure industry.

1 In the US, the average annual salary for activities coordinators is about …
a $12,000. **b** $22,000. **c** $32,000.

2 … is NOT usually a requirement for an activities coordinator.
a Physical fitness **b** Teaching experience **c** Public speaking experience

3 Choose all that are true. Activities coordinators work …
a at schools. **b** at resort hotels. **c** on cruise ships. **d** at senior homes. **e** at camps.

UNIT 9 Room for Me

WHAT DO YOU ALREADY KNOW?

1 Think about where you live. Is it a house, an apartment, or something else? Write words that describe your home and what's in it.

2 IN PAIRS Share and compare your information. Add more words to your list.

Furniture

Parts of a house/rooms

DISCUSS & SHARE

VIDEO

3 IN GROUPS Watch the video and answer the question.
SYM Would you prefer to live in a house or an apartment?

In this unit, you will ...

- talk about different kinds of housing, where you prefer to live, and what houses will be like in the future.
- use thinking skills: understand and evaluate.
- read about housing solutions.
- use strategies to keep talking by asking for and giving opinions.
- use decision-making skills to plan and develop a neighborhood.
- learn tips for problem solving in group work.

LESSON 1 **Housing Solutions**

READING

A **READING SKILL—Predict** **Look at the picture and the title of the article in B. What do you think the article is about?**

B 9.01 **Read the article. Then check (✓) the correct options.**

Half-houses in Chile

In many areas, people can't **afford** to buy or **rent** a place to live. It's a problem that will become worse in the future. Some cities have found interesting solutions.

One example is half-houses in Chile. An earthquake hit the town of Constitución in 2010 and destroyed about 80% of the buildings. The local government hired an architecture firm to provide **low-cost** houses. They built houses that are only half-finished. The owners finish the house when they have the money. It means that each family can decide what they need: a garage, another bedroom, a **hall**, a **balcony**. One resident says: "We're going to build another bedroom and bathroom in two years. We can add our personal style."

Another solution is micro-units, like those at Carmel Place in New York City. These are very small apartments, around 28 square meters. They are too small for a family, but perfect for single young professionals. Each one-room apartment has the usual appliances—a stove, a refrigerator, and a microwave—and there's a room in another part of the building for washing clothes. The smart use of special furniture means the room can become a bedroom, kitchen, office, or living room. The desk becomes a dining table and the couch becomes a bed. The coffee table folds down and goes under the bed at night. A young resident says: "I'm having a friend over for dinner tonight. I just turn the bed into a **couch**, the desk into a table, and we're good to go!"

1 What are the advantages of half-houses for the city?

- ☐ They are low-cost.
- ☐ They don't collapse in an earthquake.
- ☐ They are big enough for families.
- ☐ They have a garage.
- ☐ Residents choose what to build.
- ☐ The half-houses are built in a traditional style.

2 What are the apartments like at Carmel Place?

- ☐ People can change the small space in many ways.
- ☐ They are big enough for families.
- ☐ They have a kitchen and an office in two rooms.
- ☐ There are washing machines in the apartment building.

C **THINKING SKILL—Understand** **Compare these examples to your own area. What housing programs does your area offer? Do people use these programs?**

VOCABULARY

A **Complete each sentence with a bold word from the text in READING B.**

1 Something that is ______________ is cheap, not expensive.
2 A ______________ is a place where you can stand outside a window.
3 If you can ______________ something, you have enough money for it.
4 A ______________ is a seat for two or three people.
5 The long, narrow area in a house that leads to different rooms is the ______________.
6 When you ______________ a place, you pay money each month to live there.

MAKE IT REAL

When people say they are "good to go," it means they are ready to do something, e.g. *We have popcorn, soda, and tickets for the movie. We're good to go!*

GRAMMAR future forms

A Read the article in READING B again. Underline sentences with *will*, *going to*, and the present progressive. Then read the sentence below and write if it refers to the present or the future.

1 My train leaves at nine o'clock tomorrow morning. ____________

B Complete the grammar rules with words from the box.

arrangements intentions predictions schedule

1 To make ____________ about the future, we use *will* or *going to*.
2 To talk about future ____________, we use *going to*.
3 To talk about future ____________, we use the present progressive.
4 To talk about future events that happen on a ____________, we use the simple present.

For more practice, go to page 154.

C Choose the correct option.

1 **I rent** / **'m going to rent** an apartment downtown next year.
2 **I meet** / **am meeting** my friend tomorrow at 9 a.m.
3 Do you think you **will rent** / **are renting** an apartment in the future?
4 What **do you do** / **are you going to do** this weekend?
5 My new job **starts** / **will starting** next month, and I need to find somewhere to live.

D IN PAIRS Ask and answer the questions.

1 What fun things are you doing this week?
2 What are you going to do this weekend?
3 When does your next vacation start? What are you going to do?

SPEAKING

A Check (✓) the housing problems your neighborhood or city faces. Then add more ideas.

- ☐ Rents are high.
- ☐ Houses/apartments are expensive.
- ☐ There aren't enough places to live.
- ☐ The construction isn't good.
- ☐ Houses/apartments are too small.
- ☐ ____________________________

B How do you think your neighborhood or city is going to change over the next five years? Choose if you *Agree* or *Disagree*. Add two more ideas.

1 Companies or the government are going to build many more houses or apartment buildings. Agree / Disagree
2 Young people will move to other areas to live. Agree / Disagree
3 Companies or the government will build cheaper places to live. Agree / Disagree
4 ____________________________ Agree / Disagree
5 ____________________________ Agree / Disagree

C IN PAIRS Discuss the questions. Use the Confident Communicator box to help you.

1 What are some problems with housing in your area?
2 How do you think housing will change in your area?

CONFIDENT COMMUNICATOR
KEEP TALKING

Use the following expressions to ask for opinions.

What do you think? *What about you?*
What's your opinion? *Do you agree?*

LESSON 2

I Might Live Downtown

VOCABULARY living together

A Complete the sentences with words from the box.

apartment hunting	live alone	roommate	share the chores
housemate	rent a room	share the bills	studio apartment

1 I'm going to go ______________ this afternoon. I want to find a place to live.
2 You share a house with a ______________, but you share a room or an apartment with a ______________.
3 You ______________ if you don't live with other people.
4 When you live in a house that you share with other people, you ______________ in a house.
5 When people ______________ and ______________, they pay for things together, and they take turns doing the chores.
6 A ______________ is an apartment with one room and a bathroom.

MAKE IT YOURS

Do you live in an apartment, a house, or a townhouse? Search online or use a dictionary to find the right words and phrases.

B IN PAIRS Would you rather live alone or have roommates? Discuss. Explain why using the phrases from A.

LISTENING

A 9.02 LISTENING SKILL—Listen for attitude Listen to two people talking. Choose the word that describes each person's attitude.

1 Ashley: **a** uncertain **b** afraid **c** unhappy
2 Ethan: **a** nervous **b** excited **c** uninterested

B 9.02 Listen again and choose the correct option.

1 Ashley … living with her family.
a likes **b** doesn't like
2 Ethan's brother and his friends …
a share an apartment. **b** live near each other.
3 Ashley … to live with a friend.
a wants **b** doesn't want
4 Ethan says that … might be hard.
a finding a cheap apartment **b** traveling to work

C THINKING SKILL—Evaluate What are the advantages and disadvantages of living with a friend?

PRONUNCIATION /aʊ/ and /oʊ/

A 9.03 Write each word in the correct category. Then listen and repeat the words.

allow	found	know	own
sound	below	now	phone

1 /aʊ/ like *house*: ________ ________ ________ ________
2 /oʊ/ like *go*: ________ ________ ________ ________

GRAMMAR future possibility and certainty

A Read the sentences. Then choose the correct option.

I **might** still be at home with Mom and Dad.
You **could** live with a friend.
You **may** find something cheap outside the city.
I **probably won't** have enough money for that.
I **will definitely** miss them!

1 We use *may*, *might*, and *could* to talk about things that are **sure** / **possible** in the future.
2 We use *probably* when we are not **sure** / **almost** sure about the future.
3 We use *definitely* when we are **not sure** / **very sure** about the future.

For more practice, go to page 155.

B Read the conversations and choose the correct option.

1 A: Do you think you might live in your home town after you graduate?
B: Oh, yes! I ____________ live there. I'm sure of that.
a probably will **b** might **c** will definitely

2 A: Do you think you'll live in another city in the future?
B: Maybe, but I ____________. I'm not sure.
a might not **b** could not **c** won't

3 A: Do you think you might live in another country one day?
B: Well, I guess I ____________ get a job in another country. I don't know.
a will **b** may not **c** could

4 A: What kind of place do you think you might live in after you graduate?
B: I ____________ have enough money for a house, so I might rent a small apartment.
a may not **b** could not **c** might

C IN PAIRS Talk about future possibilities. Finish the sentences and ask each other questions.

1 This evening, I might … 2 Tomorrow, I may … 3 This weekend, I'll probably …

SPEAKING

A Rate how likely each possibility is for you in the future: 1 (*definitely won't*), 2 (*probably won't*), 3 (*may, might, could*), 4 (*probably will*), or 5 (*definitely will*).

live in a small town ____
live in another country ____
live in the center of a big city ____
live in a house with a yard ____
live with your parents ____
live with other family members ____
live in an apartment building ____
live with a friend ____

B IN PAIRS Talk about where you might live in the future. Ask questions about your predictions. Use the Confident Communicator box to help you.

A: I'll probably live in another country for a few years. *B: Why is that?*
A: I might get a job and …

CONFIDENT COMMUNICATOR
KEEP TALKING

Use the following expressions to ask for reasons for opinions.
Why is that?
Why do you think that?
Why do you say that?

The Future of Houses

VOCABULARY appliances

A IN PAIRS Choose the three things you think might change most in the future. Discuss how you think they might change.

1 **air conditioner**

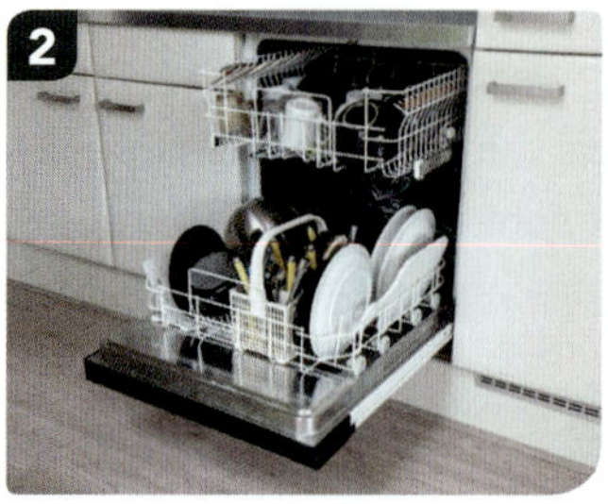
2 **dishwasher**

3 **solar panel**

4 **lighting**

5 **kitchen stove**

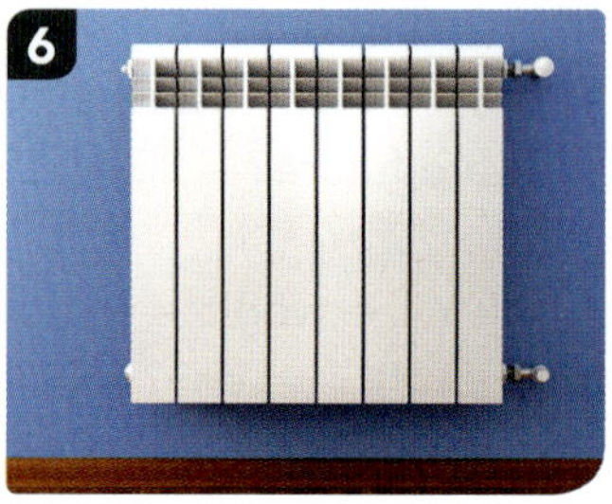
6 **heater**

7 **washing machine**

B IN PAIRS Discuss the question and check the meanings of the words and phrases in bold.

How can **sunlight** help us **save energy** and **save money**?

LISTENING

A You are going to listen to a talk. Look at the picture and say what you think the talk is about.

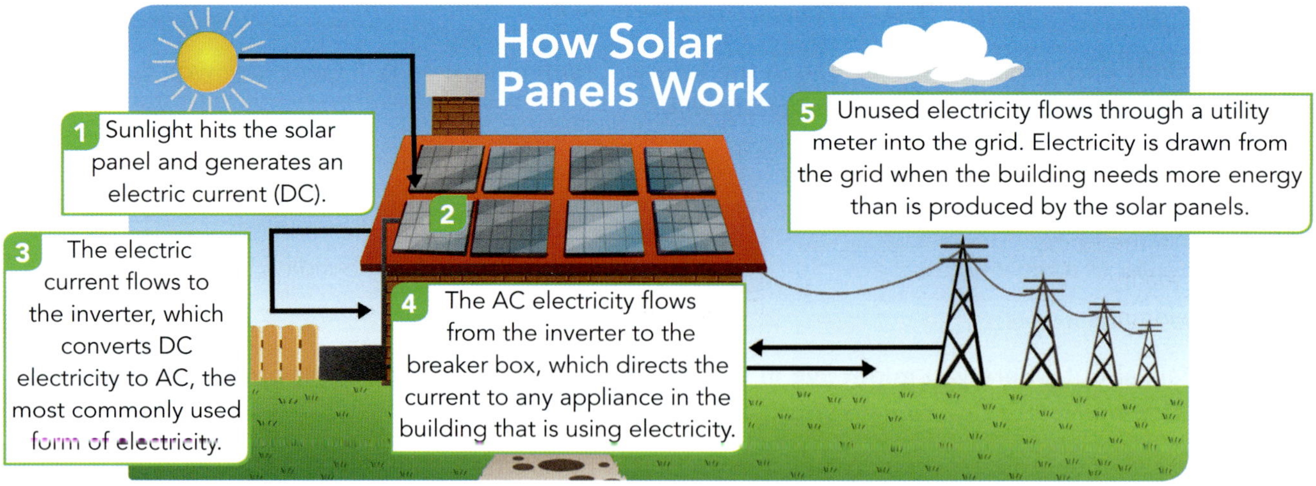

B 9.04 LISTENING SKILL—Take notes Listen to a talk and complete the notes.

solar panels
- receive **1** ______________ on sunny days
- create **2** ______________ from special materials

inverter
- takes DC current from the **3** ______________
- sends AC current to the **4** ______________

electricity grid
- takes electricity that the house **5** ______________
- provides power when there is **6** ______________

C THINKING SKILL—Evaluate How can we persuade more people to use solar power?

WRITING

A Read the article and answer the question.

Future Homes

What will the homes of tomorrow be like? I think we'll see big changes in entertainment. For example, homes will have 3D movie theaters with amazing sound. We might have virtual reality in some homes. I don't think that will be very popular because it will be expensive. There could also be big changes in the kitchen. For instance, you might choose a recipe and the stove will know how to cook it. It will tell you when your food is ready. Finally, parts of your house will change. Take windows, for example. They might go dark automatically at night to help you sleep. Or the windows might show messages to people at your door. Houses are going to change in many ways, and I can't wait!

According to the writer, what changes might we see in entertainment, in kitchens, and in windows?

____

B Choose the correct option.

1. The way we use energy will change. **As** / **For** example, all houses will have solar panels.
2. Rooms will change. **One** / **For** instance, houses might have a special room just for virtual reality.
3. Some rooms will change. **Take** / **Look** bathrooms, for example. We will use much less water.

C Choose three things you think are going to be different in our homes. In your notebook, write the main way you think each one is going to be different.

robots: They will clean our homes.

D Write a paragraph about how you think houses might change in the future.

E IN PAIRS Share your paragraphs from D. Comment on the way your partner uses examples.

MAKE IT DIGITAL

Search online for ideas on homes of the future. Tell the class what you find.

SPEAKING

A Check (✓) the future changes in homes that you are interested in. Add your own ideas.

- ☐ robots in the home
- ☐ virtual reality
- ☐ entertainment
- ☐ use of energy
- ☐ use of water
- ☐ security

______________________ ______________________

B IN PAIRS Talk about the things that interest you about the future of homes. Give reasons for your opinions. Use the Confident Communicator box to help you.

CONFIDENT COMMUNICATOR
KEEP TALKING

Use the following expressions to give reasons for your opinions.
I think we'll have robots in the home because they can do housework for us.
The reason for that is robots will do housework for us.
That's because robots will do housework for us.

Language and Life

Decision-making – Developing a Neighborhood

A 9.05 **Read the article and answer the questions below.**

NEIGHBORHOOD DEVELOPMENT

Neighborhoods are changing all the time. That means someone has to make decisions about these changes. It might be urban planners or members of local government. They often have to decide between different plans for a neighborhood. They may have to think about costs, housing, and the needs of local people. How do they make their decisions?

One tool to help planners make a decision is a decision matrix. In a decision matrix, they list the important results they want for the neighborhood. For example, local people may want more houses, less traffic, or more parks. Planners develop several plans to get these results. They then score each plan against each result: –2 for a very negative effect, –1 for a negative effect, 0 for no effect, +1 for a positive effect, and +2 for a very positive effect. The plan with the highest total score is the one to choose.

People can use a decision matrix to help with all kinds of decisions, from large business decisions to personal decisions like making a budget or planning a vacation.

	Plan A	*Plan B*	*Plan C*
Result 1			
Result 2			
Result 3			
Total			

1 Who makes decisions about how neighborhoods develop? ______

2 What is the purpose of a decision matrix? ______

B **IN GROUPS Think about people in a neighborhood you know. Look at the ideas below and add your own. Which do you think are most important to them? Choose four.**

- ☐ cheaper places to live
- ☐ more public transportation
- ☐ more stores
- ☐ ______
- ☐ more job opportunities
- ☐ more green spaces
- ☐ better quality housing
- ☐ ______

C **Write your four choices from B in the first column of the decision matrix in E.**

D **IN PAIRS Read the plans for neighborhood development and discuss which one you prefer.**

Plan A

The city is going to build a number of apartment buildings. Half the apartments will be available to buy and half will be available to rent. The apartments will be different sizes. The first floor of each apartment building will be for stores.

Plan B

The city is going to knock down some houses and build a park. They will clean up the area, and the park will have a playground and a picnic area. There will also be basketball courts and other sports facilities.

Plan C

The city is going to build a large mall. There will be a small number of apartments for rent in the mall. The mall will include large and small stores, together with restaurants and a movie theater. A new bus route will connect downtown with the mall.

E **IN PAIRS Score each plan from D from –2 to +2 for each result.**

What our city needs	Plan A	Plan B	Plan C
Total			

F **IN PAIRS Add up the total score for each plan and write it in the table in E. Your preferred plan is the one with the highest score. Complete the list.**

First choice: Plan _____
Second choice: Plan _____
Third choice: Plan _____

MAKE IT DIGITAL

Search online for "plans for development" in your city or a city near you.

G **IN GROUPS Compare your results from F and explain your thinking.**

H **Discuss the questions.**

1 How useful was the decision matrix?
2 In what other situations do you think the decision matrix would help?

VOCABULARY review

SCORE: / 10

A Complete the text with the words from the box.

air conditioner	balcony	hall	solar panels	studio apartment
apartment hunting	couch	roommate	stove	washing machine

This month, I have to go **1** ________ to find a new place to live. I want an apartment with built-in appliances: a **2** ________ to wash my clothes, a **3** ________ to cook on, and an **4** ________ to keep the air cool. I want **5** ________ to get energy from the sun. I'd like to have a small **6** ________ inside the front door, and a **7** ________ to sit outside. I don't need much furniture because right now I have a small **8** ________ . I have a nice **9** ________ that becomes a bed. I have a small desk and two chairs, and that's it. I'd like to get a bigger apartment, but then I'd need to find a **10** ________ to share the bills.

GRAMMAR review

SCORE: / 10

A Choose the correct option. If both answers are correct, choose both.

1. Do you think your neighborhood **is getting** / **will get** better in the future?
2. Tomorrow morning, I **am going** / **go** apartment hunting with a friend.
3. Where **do you live** / **are you going to live** when you graduate?
4. I think I **will rent** / **am renting** an apartment downtown when I get a job.
5. Our new housemate **is arriving** / **arrives** tomorrow from his hometown.

B Complete the sentences with the correct expression of future possibility or certainty.

1. I want a studio apartment, but I ________ have enough money for one.
2. I ________ go back and live with my parents for a few months. I haven't decided.
3. If I don't find a job, I definitely ________ be able to afford my own place.
4. I guess I ________ live in another country one day. Who knows?
5. My friends and I are sure we ________ rent a house together.

16–20 correct: You can talk about living situations and appliances. You can talk about future possibilities and certainty.
0–15 correct: Look again at the Vocabulary and Grammar sections in the unit.

TOTAL SCORE: / 20

WHAT DO YOU KNOW NOW? Look back at page 87 and add the words you know now to the boxes.

STUDY SKILLS PROBLEM SOLVING

A Take the quiz. Then go to **Study Skills** on page 135. Find the answers and learn more about problem solving.

1 Why is problem solving a useful skill to develop? Choose all the answers that apply.

a It can help you to improve your research skills.
b It can activate your knowledge on a subject.
c It helps you to develop your creativity.

2 Choose all the ways that a team can solve a problem.

a Brainstorm ideas to get different ways of looking at the problem.
b The leader of the project should make all the decisions so the team can work well.
c Research similar problems and solutions.

UNIT 10

Wellbeing

WHAT DO YOU ALREADY KNOW?

1 Think about words that describe your health.

2 **IN PAIRS** Share and compare your ideas. Add more words to your list.

Food

Exercise

VIDEO

DISCUSS & SHARE

3 **IN GROUPS** Watch the video and answer the question.

SYM Which is more important for good health, nutrition or exercise?

In this unit, you will ...

- talk about brain power, accidents, and illnesses, and improving fitness.
- use thinking skills: brainstorm, evaluate, and understand.
- read about brain power.
- use strategies to start and keep talking by agreeing and disagreeing, asking about an illness, and making a statement stronger.
- use critical thinking skills to develop an ad campaign to improve public health.
- follow a family physician to learn about this job and the skills needed for the health care industry.

LESSON 1 Power Up Your Brain!

READING

A As a class, say if each statement is true for you. Explain why or why not.

1 I generally eat well.

2 I generally get enough sleep.

B READING SKILL—Scan Read the article quickly and check (✓) the ideas it mentions.

- ☐ healthy food
- ☐ learning an instrument
- ☐ making decisions
- ☐ doing well in school
- ☐ taking a break

3 WAYS to POWER UP YOUR BRAIN!

How can you help your brain work better? Here is some advice from the experts.

• Get healthy

One way to help your **brain** is to get healthy by exercising more and eating better. In one study, people had a better **memory** after six weeks of physical training. Some studies found that if you exercise for 10 minutes before thinking about a problem, it improves your problem-solving and decision-making skills. Your **diet** is also important. Vitamins and minerals from food—like fish, vegetables, and **nuts**—help keep your brain healthy.

• Sleep better

Sleep isn't just rest for the body. It also rests your brain. During sleep, your brain organizes your **experiences**, often through dreams. When you are learning new skills, you actually get better at them while you sleep! Sleep helps you think clearly while you're awake. Most people who sleep only four to six hours in one night don't think clearly the next day.

• Keep learning

Your brain can change, something known as neuroplasticity. If you challenge your brain, it will develop more connections between its **neurons**. One thing you can do to challenge your brain is to learn a new skill, such as a new language or a musical instrument. Some people enjoy brain training—online sites and apps that use **puzzles** or other tasks to exercise your brain. Many of these sites and apps don't have much effect on the brain, and they certainly won't make you more **intelligent**. However, psychologists have created some types of puzzles that make your brain work faster. Doing these tasks makes some people feel sharper in their everyday lives.

C 10.01 Read the article in B again and answer the questions.

1 How might you improve your decision-making skills? ____________

2 What happens to most people after only getting four to six hours sleep? ____________

3 Does brain training work? ____________

D THINKING SKILL—Brainstorm What are other ways you could develop your brain?

VOCABULARY

A Complete each sentence with a bold word from the text in READING B.

1 Your ____________ is all the things you usually eat.

2 Your ____________ are the things that happen to you each day.

3 ____________ are games or tasks where you have to think carefully to find the answer.

4 ____________ are the cells in your brain.

5 If you are ____________, you are smart and you think very clearly about things.

6 Your ____________ is the organ inside your head that controls your body.

7 Your ____________ is the part of you that remembers things.

8 ____________ are the dry fruit of some trees. They have a hard shell.

GRAMMAR zero and first conditional

A Read the sentences. Then choose the correct answer.

Zero conditional

If someone sleeps more, his or her brain works better.
if clause — result clause

First conditional

If you start learning a new skill, your brain will work faster.
if clause — result clause

1 The zero conditional expresses **general facts and scientific truths / real possibilities in the present or future.**
2 The first conditional expresses **general facts and scientific truths / real possibilities in the present or future.**

For more practice, go to page 156.

B Circle the verbs in each clause of the sentences in A. Then complete the grammar rules.

Zero conditional

1 In the *if* clause, use the ____________ tense.
2 In the result clause, use the ____________ tense.

First conditional

3 In the *if* clause, use the ____________ tense.
4 In the result clause, use ____________ + base form of the verb.

C Complete the text with the correct form of words from the box.

be	get	learn	do	grow	practice

If you **1** ____________ a new skill, your brain **2** ____________. The density of white matter in your brain increases and your neurons work better. However, it has to be an active skill, such as learning the piano. You **3** ____________ better if you **4** ____________ every day. Each time you practice, you create new connections between your neurons. Play for just a short time and it makes a difference. If you **5** ____________ that for a year, you **6** ____________ amazed at your progress.

D IN PAIRS Discuss if you agree or disagree with the statements. Explain your answers.

1 You can do anything if you try hard enough.
2 If you relax and stop worrying, you will succeed.

SPEAKING

A Choose the option that you agree with the most.

1 If I study …, I learn more.
 a alone b with friends

2 I will do better on an exam if I … the night before.
 a relax b study for hours

B IN PAIRS Compare your answers from A and discuss the reasons for your choices. Explain why you don't agree with the other choices. Use the Confident Communicator box to help you.

CONFIDENT COMMUNICATOR
START TALKING

Use the following expressions to say you agree or disagree with an idea.
I agree that *it's a good idea to study with other people.*
I disagree that *it's easier to concentrate if you listen to music*

Accidents and Illnesses

VOCABULARY accidents and illnesses

A Complete the phrases with the words from the box.

ankle head throat arm leg

1 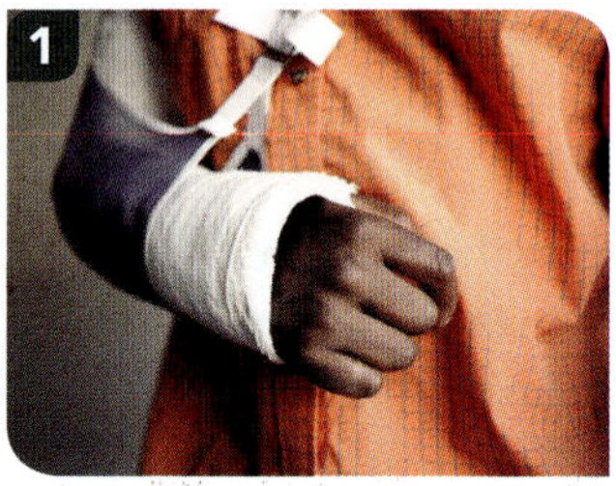

break your / have a broken ______________

2 

have a ______________ache

3 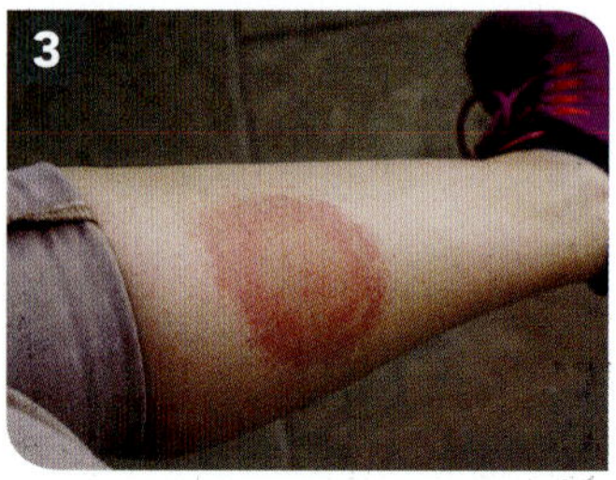

have a rash on your ______________

4 

sprain your / have a sprained ______________

5 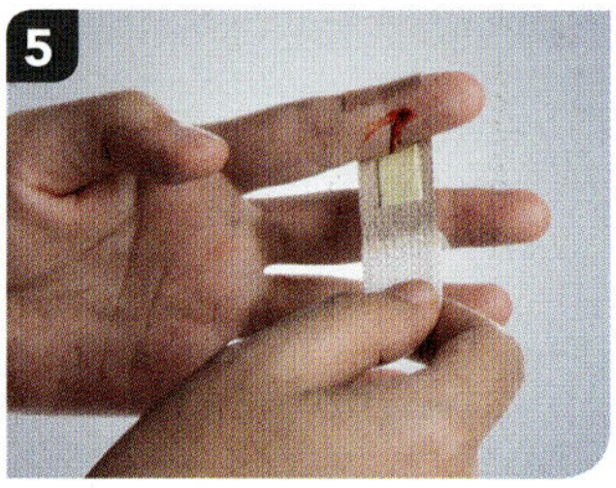

have a cut

6 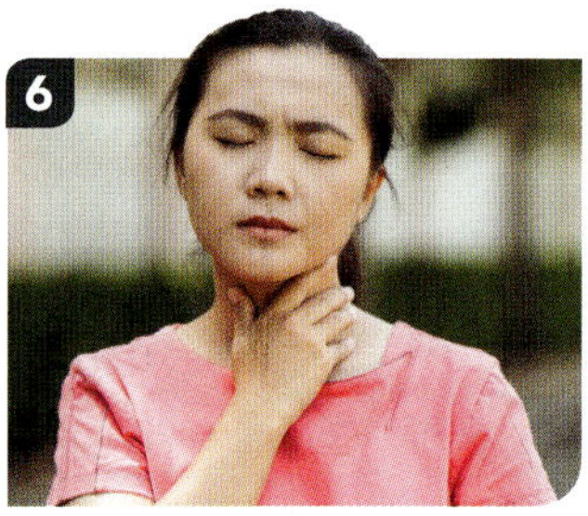

have a sore ______________

7 

have a cold

8 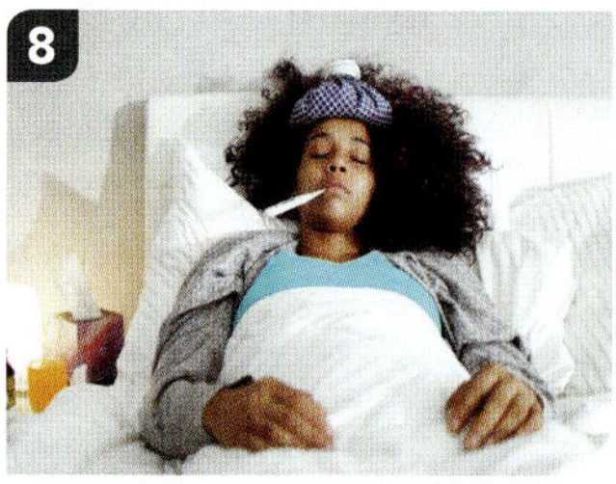

have a fever

B IN PAIRS Discuss the questions.

1 Have you ever hurt a part of your body? What happened?
2 When was the last time you felt sick?

MAKE IT YOURS

Make a list of other words you might need to talk about accidents and illnesses.

GRAMMAR second conditional

A Read the table and choose the correct option to complete the grammar rule.

Second conditional

If you broke your arm, it would / might / could be hard to drive.
if clause — result clause

1 We use the second conditional to talk about …
  a real possibilities in the present or future.
  b hypothetical or impossible situations in the present or future.

For more practice, go to page 157.

B Read the sentence. Then complete the grammar rules.

If I **broke** a bone, I **would go** to the hospital.

1 In the *if* clause, use the ______________ tense.
2 In the result clause, use ______________ + base form.

MAKE IT REAL

Note that in formal English we use *if + I/he/she/it +* ***were*** instead of *was*. However, many English speakers do not use this form anymore and simply use *was*.

C **IN PAIRS** **Discuss the questions.**

What would you do if you …

1 lost your phone? **2** won the lottery? **3** broke your leg?

LISTENING

A **10.02** **Listen to the podcast and choose *True* or *False*.**

1	Madison Gray is a doctor.	True / False
2	The right skills are very important.	True / False
3	You should help someone up right away if he or she falls.	True / False
4	You should always call an ambulance after a fall.	True / False
5	With a broken arm, you should first find something long and hard.	True / False

B **10.02 LISTENING SKILL—Listen for cause and effect** **Listen again and answer the questions.**

1 If someone was injured, and you helped the person up, what could happen?

____

2 If someone breaks an arm, why do you have to stop any bleeding first?

____

C **IN GROUPS THINKING SKILL—Evaluate** **Should we teach first aid in schools? Why or why not? Discuss.**

PRONUNCIATION intonation in conditional sentences

A **10.03** **Choose the correct intonation. Then listen and check.**

1 If I had a cough, ↗ I would buy some medicine. ↘

2 If I had a cough, ↘ I would buy some medicine. ↗

B **10.04** **Practice saying the sentences with the correct intonation.**

1 If I broke my leg, I would call an ambulance.
2 If I had a rash, I'd search for information online.
3 If I sprained my ankle, I'd ask a friend for help.

SPEAKING

A **IN PAIRS** **Read the situation and discuss your answers. Use the Confident Communicator box to help you.**

A friend who only speaks English is visiting you. How would you help your friend in each of the situations? What would you do if he or she …

- had a headache?
- had a cough and a sore throat?
- had a fever?
- had a sprained ankle?

B **IN PAIRS** **Role-play the situation in A. Student A, you are the English-speaking friend. Describe your problem. Student B, try to help Student A.**

CONFIDENT COMMUNICATOR
KEEP TALKING

Use the following phrases to ask for and give details about someone who is sick.

What's wrong?
Where does it hurt?
What's the matter?
Where do you feel pain?
I have a fever, and my head hurts.
It's not just my head. It's also my throat.

Improve Your Fitness

VOCABULARY collocations with *get*

A Complete the sentences (1–8) with *get* and a word from the box.

home	in shape	sick	tired	hungry	ready	started	upset

1 I joined a gym because I want to ______*get in shape.*______
2 I usually just turn the TV on when I ____________ from work.
3 I don't seem to have much energy, and I ____________ easily.
4 My brother is training to ____________ for the marathon next month.
5 There's a lot of work to do, so let's ____________!
6 Don't ____________. I'm sure everything will be okay.
7 I always ____________ by 10 a.m. because I don't eat breakfast.
8 When you are in bad shape, you often ____________ and take time off work.

B IN PAIRS Discuss the questions.

1 What do you usually do when you get home from class/work?
2 What are some ways people can get in shape?
3 Do you eat only at mealtimes, or do you get hungry between meals?

LISTENING

A Mark the scale with how active you are. Compare with a partner and explain.

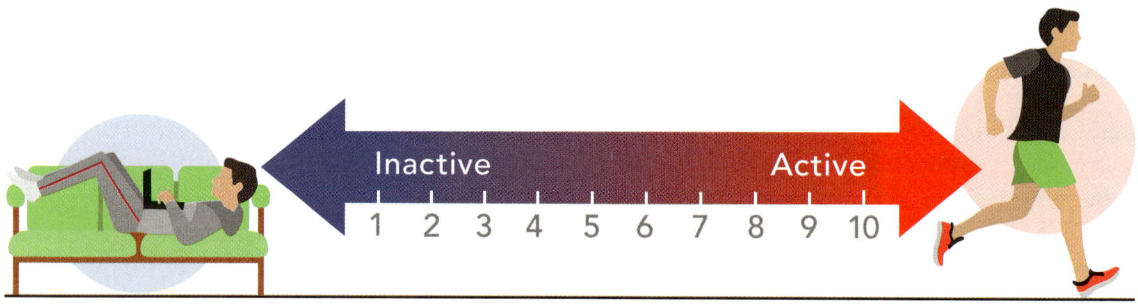

B 10.05 LISTENING SKILL—Listen for gist Check (✓) the ideas that are mentioned.

☐ This program is for people who run a lot.
☐ You need to eat well to get in shape.
☐ With Couch to 5K, you start slowly and then get faster.

C 10.05 Listen again and complete the sentences with a word or short phrase.

1 You might need to see ____________ if you have health problems.
2 In Week 1, you run for ____________.
3 You'll run for 30 minutes after ____________.
4 When you eat the right things, you don't ____________ when you're exercising.

D IN PAIRS THINKING SKILL—Understand Discuss the questions.

1 Do programs like Couch to 5K work for everyone? Why or why not?
2 Is it important to be in shape? In what ways?

WRITING

A **Read the comment from a website. In your own words, explain how Hugo got in shape.**

A small change can make a big difference! I wanted to get in shape, but I didn't have time to go to the gym. I drove to college every day, so I didn't get much exercise. One day, I decided to park my car far away from the building I needed to go to on campus, and I walked the rest of the way. Each week, I parked a little farther away. After a month, I started to feel better. After two months, people started to ask me if I was working out! There are always ways to get more exercise into your life. Why don't you try walking a little more? Start small and you'll be amazed at what you can do!

Hugo Oliveira, Curitiba, Brazil • 1 day ago

B **IN PAIRS** **Choose three small life changes you would like to try. Discuss why you would like to try them.**

- ☐ eat smaller meals
- ☐ use a fitness app
- ☐ eat at the dining table
- ☐ eat a protein-rich breakfast
- ☐ use a calorie-counting app
- ☐ stop keeping snacks at home
- ☐ drink more water
- ☐ walk instead of drive
- ☐ walk during breaks from work/class

C **Complete the sentences to persuade someone to make a change.**

1. You should ______________________________.
2. Why don't you ______________________________?
3. Have you thought about ______________________________?
4. I suggest ______________________________.

D **Imagine you made one of the small life changes in B. What happened? Write a comment for a fitness website about your experience.**

SPEAKING

A **Check (✓) the problems that keep you from getting completely in shape and healthy. Then add your own ideas.**

- ☐ not enough money
- ☐ not interested
- ☐ can't cook
- ☐ no gyms near me
- ☐ don't like sports
- ☐ don't know about healthy eating

______________________________ ______________________________

B **For each problem you checked in A, imagine what you would do if that problem didn't exist. Make notes in your notebook.**

There are no gyms near me. If there were a gym near me, I would join and start exercising.

C **IN PAIRS** **Discuss the problems from A and what you would do if they didn't exist. Use the Confident Communicator box to help you.**

CONFIDENT COMMUNICATOR
START TALKING

Use *really* to make a statement stronger.

I was ***really*** *out of shape, so I started playing tennis.*

It was a ***really*** *small change, but it helped a lot.*

Language and Life

Critical Thinking – Improving Public Health

A 10.06 **Read the article and choose the correct option.**

Many countries face serious public health problems. One example is obesity. According to the Organisation for Economic Co-operation and Development, one in two adults and nearly one in six children in its member countries are overweight or obese. That puts pressure on health services. Some countries are looking at ways of improving public health.

One way is to encourage people to eat better. Some countries, such as the United States and the United Kingdom, have five-a-day campaigns. They tell people that they should eat five portions of fruit or vegetables each day. Many countries have laws about labels on food. Producers have to show the amount of fat, protein, and carbohydrates in each food. Some countries have a "traffic light" system. Green means the food has a small amount of fat, sugar, and salt. Yellow means the food has a medium amount. Red means there's a high amount of fat, sugar, or salt. The labels help people make better choices.

Public health departments are always looking for new ideas to improve public health.

1. About __________ of all adults are overweight or obese in OECD countries.
   a a third **b** a sixth **c** half
2. Obesity causes problems for __________.
   a all countries **b** health services **c** mainly children
3. Some countries say you should eat __________ each day.
   a no more than five meals **b** five types of vegetable **c** five servings of fruit and vegetables
4. In a "traffic light" system, you can eat less fat if you choose a label where the fat is in __________.
   a green **b** yellow **c** red

B **Check the brainstorming tips you have used.**

- ☐ Suggest as many ideas as you can.
- ☐ Accept all ideas, useful and not useful, and write them down.
- ☐ Make sure everyone in your group offers an idea.
- ☐ Go online and quickly look at other people's ideas.
- ☐ Try to put ideas together and see what happens.
- ☐ Look at a problem from different points of view.

C **IN GROUPS** Brainstorm ways you could help the public health department improve the health of each of the people. Make notes of all your ideas.

a child

a young adult

a senior citizen

1 **Child:** *ban cartoon characters from unhealthy food packaging*

2 **Young adult:** *create a cool fitness app*

3 **Senior citizen:** *provide low-cost, simple, healthy recipes*

D **IN GROUPS** Choose one age group. Look at your ideas. Cross out ideas you think wouldn't work. Explain why.

If we banned cartoon characters from unhealthy food packaging, children would still want that kind of food.

E **IN GROUPS** Choose your best ideas. Explain why those ideas would work.

Idea 1: ____________________

Idea 2: ____________________

Idea 3: ____________________

F **IN GROUPS** Present your ideas to the class. Predict what would happen if the public health department used your idea.

If we created a cool fitness app for young adults, they would want to get more exercise.

G **Discuss the questions.**

1 Why is it important to consider different points of view?
2 In what other situations do you need to think critically and creatively?

MAKE IT DIGITAL

Research ways public health officials in your country are working to solve your country's most serious health problems.

VOCABULARY review

SCORE: / 10

A Complete the sentences. The first letter of the missing words is given.

Ella: Oh, Frank! You have a **1** b__________ arm! How did you do that?

Frank: I was trying to get **2** i__________ s__________ and I changed my **3** d__________ so that I was eating better.

Ella: Oh, yes. I remember.

Frank: Well, it wasn't working well, so I decided to try skateboarding. I'm a beginner, but I tried to do a few tricks. That wasn't very **4** i__________. In fact, it was kind of stupid. It was going OK, but then I got **5** t__________ and made a mistake. I fell on my arm! I had to go to the hospital.

Ella: That's awful!

Frank: The next day, after I got **6** h__________ from the hospital, I got **7** s__________. I had a temperature of 100 degrees, and I had a **8** s__________ throat. I had a **9** f__________!

Ella: Oh, no! I hope you didn't get **10** u__________!

Frank: Nah. It was fine. But I'm looking forward to getting back on my skateboard!

GRAMMAR review

SCORE: / 10

A Match the sentence beginnings (1–5) to the sentence endings (a–e). Write the letter.

1 If you eat better, ____
2 If you buy less candy, ____
3 You probably exercise more ____
4 It's possible to run 5K ____
5 If you don't have a personal trainer, ____

a if you live close to a gym.
b you will have more energy.
c you might not do the exercises correctly.
d if you run a little farther each week.
e you won't have so many problems with your teeth!

B Complete the sentences with verbs in the correct tense. Add any other words you need.

1 What __________ (you/cook) if you wanted to help your family lose weight?
2 I __________ (go) to the gym more often if I had more time.
3 If people __________ (eat) five portions of fruit and vegetables a day, there would be less obesity.
4 You'd get more exercise if you __________ (walk) to class instead of driving.
5 If I __________ (have) more money, I would probably join a gym.

16–20 correct: You can use collocations with *get* and talk about accidents and illnesses.
You can recognize zero, first, and second conditionals.
0–15 correct: Look again at the Vocabulary and Grammar sections in the unit.

TOTAL SCORE: / 20

WHAT DO YOU KNOW NOW? Look back at page 97 and add the words you know now to the boxes.

FOLLOW A PRO HEALTH CARE

Take the quiz about the medical profession. Then go to **Follow A Pro** on page 136. Find the answers and learn more about the health care industry.

1 How many doctors are there in the US?
a about 250,000 **b** about 500,000 **c** over 1 million

2 Patients with female surgeons do better than those with male surgeons.
a True **b** False

3 Where was the first hospital in North America built?
a Toronto **b** New York **c** Mexico City

UNIT 11

Use and Reuse

WHAT DO YOU ALREADY KNOW?

1 Think of words you know about recycling and improving the environment. Write the words.

2 **IN PAIRS** Share and compare your information. Add more words to your lists.

Save the Earth

DISCUSS & SHARE

VIDEO

3 **IN GROUPS** Watch the video and answer the question.

SYM Which do you use, paper or plastic?

In this unit, you will ...

- talk about what things are made of, how new materials are made, and how plastic can be recycled.
- use thinking skills: brainstorm, understand, and analyze.
- read about how T-shirts are made and recycled.
- use strategies to start and keep talking by ordering steps in a process, stating who made something, and suggesting alternatives.
- use innovation skills to brainstorm ways to upcycle materials.
- learn tips about using precise language in academic writing.

LESSON 1 The Lifecycle of a T-shirt

READING

A **As a class, discuss how you think people make the following items: jeans, shoes, jewelry.**

B 11.01 **Read the article and choose the correct options.**

From Seed to T-shirt

T-shirts are a basic part of almost everyone's closet. Over two billion T-shirts are sold every year around the world. So how are they made? And where do they **end up**?

The story starts with the seed of the cotton plant. The plants are grown on large farms. The cotton is collected and sent to a factory. There, it is cleaned and made into **yarn**. The yarn is made into cloth. This is used to make T-shirts.

The T-shirts are then **transported** around the world. Just take a look at the label on one of your T-shirts and see how far it came! The T-shirts go into stores and are sold to consumers. That's you. You probably have the T-shirt for a while, and it is worn, washed, and dried again and again. When you decide to **get rid of** it, you have a few options. You might throw it in the trash. But if you knew how much of the Earth's **natural resources** go into making a T-shirt, you might think again! A lot of energy and water are used in making and washing clothes. A lot of chemicals are used in this process, too.

One option is to recycle your old T-shirts. When a T-shirt is sent to a recycling center, it is made into other things, such as cleaning cloths. Another idea is to upcycle your T-shirts. Old T-shirts are sometimes made into belts, scarves, or bags.

1 Where does the story of a T-shirt start?
   a in a factory **b** on a farm
2 What information on a T-shirt label does the writer mention?
   a the country the T-shirt comes from **b** how to wash the T-shirt
3 Where in the lifecycle do we use a lot of energy and water?
   a growing the cotton plant **b** producing and cleaning the T-shirt
4 When a T-shirt is upcycled, it might become …
   a a scarf. **b** another T-shirt.

C **READING SKILL—Understand words from context** **Find the words from the box in the text in B. Read the context and explain what you think they mean.**

consumers label upcycle

D **THINKING SKILL—Brainstorm** **What other uses for old T-shirts can you think of? Make a list in your notebook.**

VOCABULARY

A **Match the bold words from the text in READING B to the definitions (1–5).**

1 very long, thin piece of cotton or wool: ____________________
2 moved from one place to another by truck, train, or boat: ____________________
3 come to a final place or situation that is not expected: ____________________
4 things we use from the Earth, such as water, oil, or trees: ____________________
5 throw away: ____________________

GRAMMAR simple present passive

A Underline examples of the passive voice in the article in READING B.

Over two billion T-shirts are sold every year around the world.

B Choose the correct option to complete the rules for forming and using the present passive voice.

1. Use the auxiliary *be* / *have* in the simple present followed by the **simple past** / **past participle** of the verb.
2. Use the present passive to focus on the thing that **does** / **receives** the action.
3. Use the present passive when we **don't know** / **are interested in** who or what does something.
4. Use the present passive when it's **important** / **obvious or unimportant** who or what does something.

For more practice, go to page 157.

C Complete the sentences with the present passive form of the verb in parentheses.

Do you know how a notebook **1** ____________ (make)? First of all, trees **2** ____________ (cut) down. The wood from the trees **3** ____________ (turn) into paper. Color **4** ____________ (remove) from the paper to make it white. Lines **5** ____________ (print) on the paper. Glue **6** ____________ (used) to stick the pages together. Finally, a cover **7** ____________ (put) on the notebook.

D IN PAIRS Look at what you are wearing and what you have with you. Discuss what your things are made of.

A: I'm wearing a T-shirt. It's made of cotton. *B: I have a bag. It's made of plastic and metal.*

SPEAKING

A Use the prompts to write sentences in the simple present passive.

1. water / drink by the consumer ____________
2. plastic / melt to make a bottle ____________
3. oil / take from the ground ____________
4. bottle / transport to a store ____________
5. oil / make into plastic ____________
6. the bottle / recycle ____________
7. the bottle / send to landfill ____________
8. the bottle / fill with water ____________

B IN PAIRS Look at the pictures and tell your partner about the lifecycle of a plastic bottle. Use the Confident Communicator box to help you.

First, oil is taken from the ground. Then, …

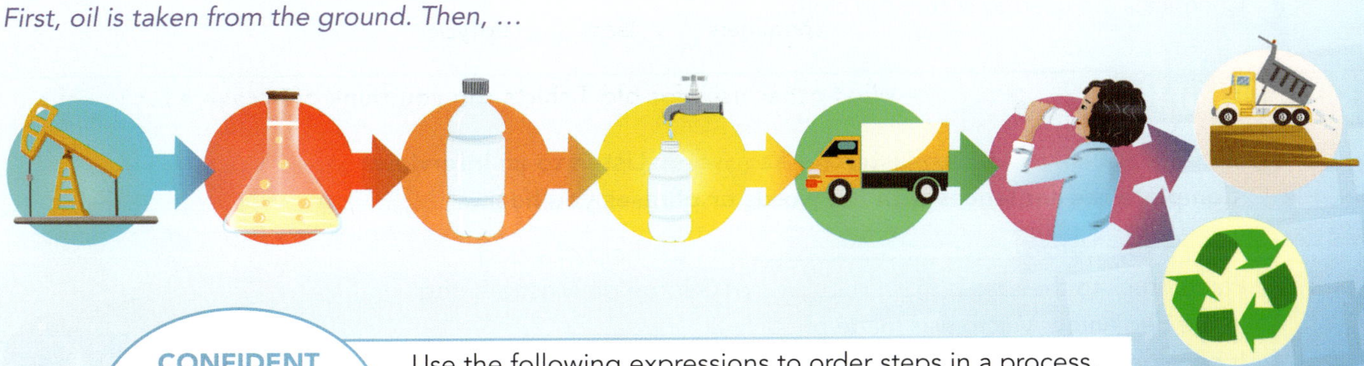

CONFIDENT COMMUNICATOR
START TALKING

Use the following expressions to order steps in a process.

First, *it's grown …*	**Next**, *it's painted …*
Then, *it's transported …*	**Finally**, *it's sold …*
After that, *it's made into …*	

LESSON 2 An Accidental Discovery

VOCABULARY clothing materials

A IN PAIRS Discuss the questions.

button

zipper

Velcro

fur

fake fur

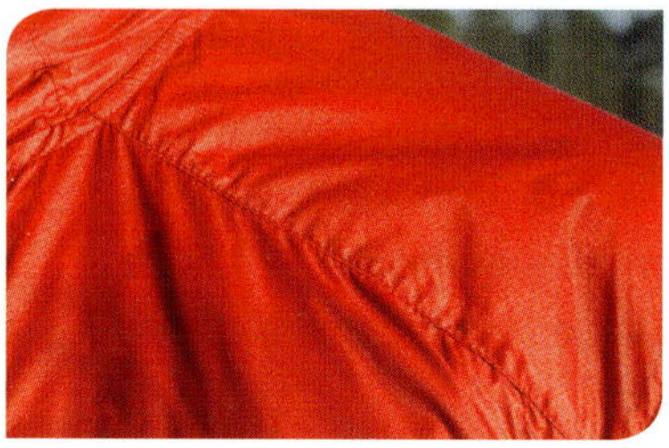

nylon

1 Do you prefer buttons, zippers, or Velcro on your clothes? Why?
2 Can you tell the difference between real and fake fur?
3 What do you think of clothes made from fur? Do you think people should wear them?
4 Do you prefer clothes made from nylon or clothes made from natural materials, such as cotton or silk? Why?

B IN PAIRS Describe how your clothes and items fasten and unfasten.

PRONUNCIATION silent *t*

A 11.02 Listen to the words. Notice that the *t* is silent.

castle whistle wrestle fasten listen soften

B 11.03 Listen to the sentences and practice saying them.

1 Listen to the way he whistles.
2 You fasten and unfasten the jacket with a zipper.
3 Chemicals are used to soften the cloth.

LISTENING

A 11.04 LISTENING SKILL—Listen for key words Listen to an interview. Complete the sentences with the words or phrases you hear.

1 Angela says Velcro ____________ with the help of a dog.
2 Plants stuck to the ____________ of George de Mestral's dog.
3 In the beginning, Velcro was made of ____________.
4 It became ____________ when it was used by astronauts.
5 In the 1980s, Velcro was used on ____________ sneakers.

B 🔊 **11.04 Listen again and choose *True* or *False*.**

1 George de Mestral was looking for plants while he was walking his dog. True / False
2 The burrs had hooks that caught onto his pants. True / False
3 De Mestral soon produced a commercial product. True / False
4 In the beginning, Velcro was used on clothes and bags. True / False
5 Velcro was used on sneakers in the 1970s. True / False

C IN PAIRS THINKING SKILL—Understand Explain why NASA used Velcro in the 1960s.

GRAMMAR simple past passive

A Read the sentences. Choose the correct option to complete the grammar rules.

De Mestral noticed that his dog **was covered** in burrs. His pants **were** also **covered** in them.

1 We form the simple past passive with the verb ***be*** / ***have*** in the simple past followed by the **past participle** / ***–ing*** *form* of the verb.
2 We use the simple past passive when we are talking about the past and …
- we want to focus on the thing that **does** / **receives** the action.
- we **are interested in** / **don't know** who or what does something.
- it's **unimportant** / **essential** who or what does something.

For more practice, go to page 158.

MAKE IT DIGITAL

Search online for the history of an invention (cell phone, TV, the internet, etc.). Find out how it was invented. Tell the class.

B Complete the text with the simple past passive form of the verbs in parentheses.

Superglue **1** ______________ (discover) by accident. In 1942, Dr. Harry Coover was trying to make clear plastic. This **2** ______________ (need) for military equipment. A number of chemicals **3** ______________ (create) in the laboratory, and one of them was called cyanoacrylate. It wasn't a clear plastic, but it was a strong glue. It **4** ______________ (develop) because it wasn't useful for that project. Nine years later, Coover was working on jet planes and cyanoacrylate **5** ______________ (use) again. This time, Coover realized how useful it was. Superglue **6** ______________ (release) as a commercial product in 1958.

SPEAKING

A Answer the questions for you.

1 Think of something that was bought for, made for, or given to you. What was it? ______________
2 When was it bought/made/given? ______________
3 Who was it bought/made/given by? ______________
4 How did you feel when it was bought/made/given? ______________

B IN PAIRS Discuss your object from A. Ask and answer questions about it. Use the Confident Communicator box to help you.

A: I have a guitar. It was bought for me by my grandfather.
B: When was it bought for you?
A: A year ago. It was given to me for my birthday, and …

CONFIDENT COMMUNICATOR
KEEP TALKING

Use *by* to say who or what did something in the passive.
It was made by my uncle.

LESSON 3 Using and Reusing Plastic

LISTENING

A **You are going to listen to a lecture. Look at the picture. What do you think the lecture will be about?**

B **11.05 LISTENING SKILL—Listen for gist** **Listen to the first part of the lecture and choose the correct summary.**

1 Thato faces a number of problems. She works in a school that has no electricity. The children are tired after their trip to school. They find it hard to do their schoolwork.

2 Thato thought about the problems of schoolchildren. Getting to and from school is sometimes dangerous. They live without electricity and it is difficult for them to do their homework.

C **11.06** **Listen to the rest of the lecture. Then complete the sentences with the words from the box.**

a light	drivers	plastic bags	schoolbags

1 There is a problem with ______________ in South Africa.
2 Thato made ______________ out of trash.
3 Her products have a solar panel, a battery, and ______________.
4 The children can be seen by ______________.

D **THINKING SKILL—Analyze** **Categorize the materials from the box.**

aluminum	ceramic	cotton	leather	plastic	steel
cardboard	copper	glass	nylon	rubber	

1 can be recycled easily: ______________________________
2 can't be recycled easily: ______________________________

VOCABULARY collocations connected to materials

A **Match the phrases (1–4) to the definitions (a–d). Write the letter.**

1 cause pollution _____
2 harm wildlife _____
3 last a long time _____
4 reduce the amount we use _____

a stay in the environment for years
b have a bad effect on animals
c use less
d have a bad effect on the environment

B **IN PAIRS** **Discuss the questions.**

1 What materials cause pollution where you live?
2 Does the pollution in your area harm wildlife?
3 What materials last a long time in the environment?
4 Do you think people should reduce the amount of plastic they use?

MAKE IT YOURS

Are there any materials around you that you don't know the English word for? Look online or in a dictionary and find out.

WRITING

A Read the email and answer the questions.

New Message

To: supporter@mail.co — Cc Bcc

Subject: Spread the Word

Dear Supporter,
Thank you for supporting Use Less Plastic. We rely on people like you to get the message out that we need to reduce the amount we use. Plastic lasts in the environment for thousands of years and harms wildlife.
We're writing to you now to ask for your help. We want you to send an email to your local news website to explain why we need to Use Less Plastic. Explain that plastic causes pollution. And remember to tell them what we can all do to Use Less Plastic.
We need to educate people about this problem to solve it.
Sincerely,
The Use Less Plastic Team

Send

1 Who does the Use Less Plastic team want you to write to? ______
2 What three things do they want you to mention? ______

B Choose the correct option.

1 The … for this is that we use too much plastic.
a result **b** reason **c** fact
2 This is … we use too much plastic.
a since **b** result **c** because
3 We are responsible for this problem … we use too much plastic.
a since **b** reason **c** why

C IN PAIRS Complete the notes.

1 Main causes of plastic pollution: plastic bags, ______
2 Problems it causes: trash in the streets, ______
3 How to use less plastic: reuse plastic bags, ______

D In your notebook, write an email to your local news website to explain why people need to use less plastic.

SPEAKING

A Think about your own use of plastic. Answer for you.

1 How many of these things do you buy or use each week?
drinks in plastic bottles: ____ drinking straws: ____
drinks in to-go cups: ____ (other) ______ : ____
items in plastic packaging: ____
2 Add up your weekly score and multiply it by 52. Write your annual total plastic items here: ______

B IN PAIRS Compare your scores and discuss how you could use less plastic. Use the Confident Communicator box to help you.

CONFIDENT COMMUNICATOR
START TALKING

Use *One / Another option is* + *to* infinitive to suggest alternatives.
***One option is to** use a refillable drinking bottle.*
***Another option is to** take your own bags to the store.*

Language and Life

Innovation – Upcycling Projects

A **11.07 Read the article and list the examples of upcycling that are mentioned.**

plant containers made from old rubber boots

upcycled art by Tim Noble and Sue Webster
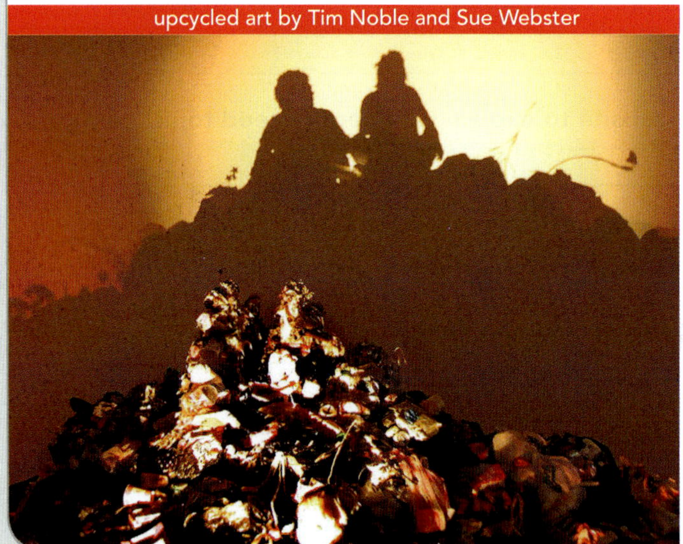

UPCYCLING **PROJECTS**

We humans use a lot of materials. Take plastic, for example.

According to Statista, every year, around 350 million metric tons of plastic are produced around the world. Sadly, not much of it is recycled. In fact, about half of the plastic is used just once and is then sent to a landfill, according to Plastic Oceans International. In 2007, Charles Fishman of *Fast Company Magazine* reported that a million plastic bottles are bought every minute of every day in the US, but only around 23% are recycled. Four trillion plastic bags are produced each year, and only 1% are recycled, according to Waste Management. Our use of other plastics is not much better. Plastic use is a big problem.

Many people are looking at ways to upcycle different materials. Upcycling involves finding new uses for materials at the end of their original use. In one project, a greenhouse was created using old plastic water bottles. In others, large coffee cans or old rubber boots were turned into containers for plants, and old rubber tires became notebook covers. Artists, too, upcycle materials. Tim Noble and Sue Webster, two British artists, create what look like piles of trash. When a light shines on the trash from a certain angle, it makes an interesting shadow on the wall.

These days institutions such as colleges and companies are looking for smarter ways to use materials. This involves reducing the amount of materials they use and thinking of ways to upcycle materials so that they last a long time.

B **IN GROUPS Read the situation and discuss the questions.**

Your college supports a local upcycling campaign. They want to encourage people to upcycle more. They want students to suggest interesting ways to upcycle. Here are the main problems the college wants to solve:

1. Students use a lot of plastic water bottles. They create trash and many of them go to the landfill. Are there ways they could be upcycled?
2. The college receives a lot of deliveries every day, which means there are a lot of cardboard boxes. They are usually recycled, but that uses energy. Are there ways they could be upcycled?

C **Write about plastic and cardboard waste at your school or workplace.**

1 Estimate how many plastic bottles are thrown out every day.

____

2 Estimate how much cardboard is thrown away each week.

____

D **Brainstorm ways of upcycling. Write as many ideas as you can.**

1 Ideas for plastic bottle reuse and upcycling

use plastic bottles as plant containers

____

____

2 Ideas for cardboard reuse and upcycling

use boxes to store books

____

____

E **Choose your best two ideas from D and add more detail. How will your idea work? Who will do it?**

Idea 1:

____

____

____

Idea 2:

____

____

____

F **Tell the class about your ideas from E.**

G **What are your favorite ideas? Take a class vote.**

H **Discuss the questions.**

1 Did working in a group help you imagine new ideas?

2 In what other situations do you need to innovate to solve problems?

MAKE IT DIGITAL

Search online to see if any of your ideas from **E** are available online, and find more ideas for ways to upcycle other products.

VOCABULARY review

SCORE: / 10

A Unscramble and write the word in parentheses.

1. Many jackets are fastened with a __________ (ppzeir).
2. We need to use fewer natural __________ (oseercus).
3. I can't __________ (snnefatu) my jacket.
4. I'm trying to __________ (deecru) the amount of plastic I use.
5. Are your socks made of __________ (lnyno)?
6. A __________ (otubnt) came off my shirt!
7. I need __________ (rayn) to make a sweater.
8. Plastic causes a lot of __________ (inltolpou).
9. Does waste harm __________ (leliiwdf) in your area?
10. The __________ (eblla) says "Made in China."

GRAMMAR review

SCORE: / 10

A Complete the sentences with the present passive form of words in the box.

add make make take wear

Sweaters **1** __________ of wool. The wool **2** __________ from sheep. It **3** __________ into yarn. Color **4** __________ to the yarn, and it is knitted into sweaters. Sweaters **5** __________ during cold weather.

B Rewrite the sentences in the passive.

1. My uncle bought this bag for me.
   ____
2. Did the Chinese invent paper?
   ____
3. Someone discovered penicillin by accident.
   ____
4. People first used CDs for music in 1982.
   ____
5. They didn't use plastic 150 years ago.
   ____

16–20 correct: You can use collocations with materials and describe clothing materials. You can use simple present passive and simple past passive.
0–15 correct: Look again at the Vocabulary and Grammar sections in the unit.

TOTAL SCORE: / 20

WHAT DO YOU KNOW NOW? Look back at page 107 and add the words you know now to the box.

STUDY SKILLS USING PRECISE LANGUAGE IN ACADEMIC WRITING

Take the quiz. Then go to **Study Skills** on page 137. Find the answers and learn more about using precise language in academic writing.

1. **It's natural for people to enjoy spending time outdoors. This statement is …**
   a a fact. **b** an opinion.
2. **A lot of people were killed in the earthquake. This statement is …**
   a precise. **b** imprecise.
3. **Eighty-five percent of people in the US go to work by car. This statement is …**
   a precise. **b** imprecise.
4. **About 150,000 people are employed by this company. This statement uses …**
   a the active voice. **b** the passive voice.

UNIT 12 I'm a Member

WHAT DO YOU ALREADY KNOW?

1 Think about your social life and the activities you like to do with other people. Write the words.

2 IN PAIRS Share and compare your ideas. Add more words to your lists.

Social life

DISCUSS & SHARE

VIDEO

3 IN GROUPS Watch the video and answer the question.

SYM Do you prefer to have friends who are similar to you or different from you?

In this unit, you will ...

- talk about types of communities, networking, and youth subcultures.
- use thinking skills: analyze and understand.
- read about the different types of social groups.
- use strategies to start and keep talking by making guesses, showing certainty, and adding a further point.
- use media literacy skills to design an ad campaign to reach a target group.
- follow an entrepreneur to learn about this job and the skills needed for the business field.

READING

A **Do you belong to a club or other social group? If so, what activities do you do in this group? Discuss as a class.**

B **12.01 READING SKILL—Understand the main ideas** **Read the article. Then match the sentence halves.**

TYPES of COMMUNITY

We all **belong** to different social groups. We choose some of them ourselves, and some of them are chosen for us. The social groups we belong to often give us support. They also say a lot about who we are and how we see ourselves.

There are many different types of community. One type is community of place. The place could be a neighborhood, a region, or a country. A second is community of interest. The people might all be interested in a certain hobby or a certain type of music, for example. A third is community of **purpose**. People in this type of community **share** the same purpose, such as learning a language or running a successful company. A fourth is community of practice. This is a group of people who share the same profession.

Each type of community can offer different things to its members. A community of place might offer people to **chat** with and to support you in difficult times. A community of interest can give you friendship and a way to learn more about a subject. A community of purpose can help you learn ways of achieving your goals. Also, people working together can often **achieve** more than a person working by himself or herself. A community of practice gives you opportunities to share ideas as well as the chance to **network**.

Any particular group might be more than one type of community. For example, a local cycling club is a community of place and a community of interest. If the members decided to raise money for a local charity, they would also be a community of purpose.

Read more

1 People in a community of place ____
2 People in a community of interest ____
3 People in a community of purpose ____
4 People in a community of practice ____

a want to achieve the same thing.
b might have the same hobby.
c might do the same job.
d might live in the same area.

C **THINKING SKILL—Analyze** **List your social groups in your notebook. Then write what type of community each of your social groups belongs to.**

VOCABULARY

A **Replace the underlined words in the sentences with synonyms from the box.**

achieve	chat	purpose of	belong to	network	share

1 You need to meet people in your profession if you want to find a better job. ____________
2 You learn more if you tell other people your ideas. ____________
3 I hope to do a lot in my career. ____________
4 I am a member of a chess club. ____________
5 The reason for our study group is to practice our English. ____________
6 I'm very busy studying, so I don't have time to sit and talk with friends. ____________

GRAMMAR reflexive pronouns

A Read the article in READING B again and complete the table.

	Subject pronouns	Reflexive pronouns
Singular	I	myself
	you	yourself
	he	**1**
	she	**2**
	it	itself
Plural	we	**3**
	you	yourselves
	they	themselves

MAKE IT REAL

Reflexive pronouns are used in many idiomatic expressions in English. Examples are *teach yourself to do something* (learn something without a teacher), *help yourself to something* (get something without the assistance of your host), and *behave yourself* (behave correctly).

B Match the functions (1–2) to the examples (a–b). Write the letter.

We use reflexive pronouns …

1 when the subject and the object of the sentence are the same. _____
2 to mean "without help from another person." _____

a *Did you start the fan club yourself or did you have help?*
b *I see myself as a professional person.*

For more practice, go to page 158.

C Complete the text with reflexive pronouns.

The way we see **1** ______________ may depend on the groups we belong to. For example, if you have a large social life, you probably consider **2** ______________ to be friendly and confident. People who belong to a sports club may think of **3** ______________ as good members of a team. This can help in their future careers. Different groups can also give you different experiences. Someone who joins a community of purpose, such as a local action group, may achieve something that he or she can't achieve by **4** ______________ or **5** ______________. If you can't find the right group, then you might think about starting one **6** ______________. This can also be an interesting experience.

PRONUNCIATION /s/ vs. /ʃ/

A 12.02 Listen and choose the word or phrase you hear.

1 self / shelf
2 yourself / your shelf
3 herself / her shelf
4 sock / shock
5 so / show
6 sign / shine

SPEAKING

A IN PAIRS Discuss the questions. Use the Confident Communicator box to help you.

1 What different communities of interest do you belong to or did you belong to in the past?
2 What do/did you enjoy the most about each different group?

CONFIDENT COMMUNICATOR
START TALKING

To talk about something when you're not completely sure or when you're still thinking about your opinion, use *I guess*:
I guess I enjoy sharing ideas with people the most.

LESSON 2 Developing Your Network

VOCABULARY networking

A Complete the sentences with words or phrases from the box.

contact	intern	job hunting	stay in touch
get to know	introduce yourself	make time for	

1 When you make friends with someone, you ____________ him or her.
2 When you say hello to someone for the first time, you ____________.
3 When you fit something into your schedule, you ____________ it.
4 An ____________ is someone who works for experience and usually isn't paid.
5 When you continue to communicate with an old friend, you ____________ with him or her.
6 When you are looking for work, you are ____________.
7 Someone you know in a profession is a ____________.

B IN PAIRS Discuss the questions.

1 Do you find it easy to introduce yourself to people and get to know them?
2 How can contacts help when you are job hunting or looking for a position as an intern?
3 Is it important to make time for old friends and stay in touch with them?

LISTENING

A Read the statement and say if you agree or disagree.

It's not what you know that's important—it's who you know.

B 12.03 LISTENING SKILL—Listen for the main ideas Listen to part of a radio show and check (✓) the advice the speaker gives.

- ☐ speak to people in your office
- ☐ speak to members of your family
- ☐ speak to old school friends
- ☐ join online groups
- ☐ research companies online
- ☐ go to career fairs
- ☐ write to companies

C 12.03 Listen again and complete the sentences with the words or short phrases you hear.

1 You can learn a lot from ____________ people in your office.
2 When you leave a job, it's a good idea to ____________ with people.
3 Ask questions, ____________, and post comments in online groups.
4 In online groups, you might be the first to hear about ____________.
5 You could ask companies about working as ____________.
6 In speed networking, you talk to each person for ____________.

D THINKING SKILL—Understand Explain how career fairs are useful.

GRAMMAR review of tenses

A Match the sentences (1–5) to the functions (a–e). Write the letter.

1. My contact **works** in the accounting department. ______
2. I **am looking for** an internship. ______
3. I **was** nervous about meeting people when I started working here. ______
4. I **was chatting** to a colleague when you called me. ______
5. **Have** you **spoken** to your friends about their career plans? ______

a a past state or habit
b an action in progress at a past moment
c a present state or habit
d an action in progress now
e an action at an unspecific time in the past

For more practice, go to page 159.

B Choose the correct option.

1. My plane … at six, so I'll be in Washington at nine.
   a leaves **b** has left **c** was leaving
2. Lola … as a waitress until she can find a job in engineering.
   a works **b** has worked **c** is working
3. I … to a speed networking event next weekend.
   a am going **b** have gone **c** go
4. If you … a professional association, you would make useful connections.
   a join **b** joined **c** have joined
5. I … in this office for six months.
   a work **b** am working **c** have worked

C Choose the correct option.

When I **1 have worked** / **was working** at my last job, I **2 was trying** / **tried** to speak to everyone in my office once a day. After I **3 was leaving** / **left** that position, I **4 was staying** / **stayed** in touch with all my colleagues. I **5 am thinking** / **think** it's important because you never **6 know** / **have known** when you might want someone's help. And it **7 has helped** / **was helping** me a number of times. Right now, I **8 am looking** / **look** for a new job, and I **9 ask** / **have asked** my contacts about job opportunities. Fingers crossed!

SPEAKING

A IN PAIRS Discuss the questions. Use the Confident Communicator box to help you.

1. What are you thinking of doing to develop your network?
2. In what ways is networking important in your chosen profession?

B Check (✓) the things you personally are thinking of doing to develop your network. Then add details and other ideas.

- ☐ speak to family members
- ☐ speak to friends
- ☐ join online groups
- ☐ contact companies directly

______________________ ______________________

CONFIDENT COMMUNICATOR
START TALKING

To say how certain you are about a plan, use *probably* (*not*) or *definitely* (*not*):
I will definitely stay in touch with my friends.
I'll probably get a job as an intern.

LESSON 3 Youth Subculture

VOCABULARY appearance

A Look at the pictures. Write the hairstyle or clothing style you think each person wears.

Hairstyle:	Clothing style:
beard mustache short/long hair color	dark/bright clothes jewelry earrings necklace tight/loose costume make-up

1 

goth

____

2 

hipster

____

3 

otaku

____

B IN PAIRS Discuss the questions.

1 Do you prefer to wear bright or dark colors?
2 Do you have a particular clothing style? Is it similar to your friends' clothing style?
3 Do you generally wear accessories? Which ones?

MAKE IT YOURS

Think of the clothes and accessories you own. Do you know the English word for all of them? Check in a dictionary and make a note of any you don't know. Describe your personal style to a classmate.

LISTENING

A IN PAIRS Have you seen people who look like the pictures in VOCABULARY A, either in real life or on TV/ online? Why do you think they dress in that style? Discuss.

B 12.04 LISTENING SKILL—Listen for gist Listen to a podcast and number the sentences in the correct order (1–4) to create a summary.

_____ Young people want to look different from their parents.
_____ Young people want to show their personality.
_____ Young people in different groups wear different clothes.
_____ Young people want to feel they belong to a group.

C 12.04 Listen again and write short answers.

1 What does the speaker say about goths?
____
2 What example of a youth subculture in the past does the speaker mention?
____
3 What might youth subcultures tell you about someone you've never met?
____

D THINKING SKILL—Understand Describe the youth subcultures that exist in your country. Discuss as a class.

WRITING a description

A Read the description and match the sentence halves. Write the letter.

One youth tribe in my country is cosplayers. A Japanese reporter invented the term *cosplay* using the words *costume* and *play* in 1984. Cosplayers are interested in video games. They create costumes based on characters from popular video games and movies. Cosplayers wear bright colors and often wear make-up to make them look like their favorite characters. They meet to show each other their colorful costumes, and they often take selfies to show people online. They often like listening to the music from video games. Personally, I think cosplayers are brave. They aren't afraid to dress like their heroes. Cosplaying is a great way to meet people with the same interests.

1 First, _____
2 Second, _____
3 Third, _____

a the writer gives his or her personal opinion.
b the writer gives background information and a little history.
c the writer describes what the people look like and what they do.

B You are going to write a description of a youth subculture. Make notes to answer the questions before you write.

1 What youth subculture are you going to write about? _____
2 What kind of clothes do they wear? _____
3 What do members do together? _____
4 Do they listen to a particular kind of music? _____
5 What is your opinion of that subculture? _____

C Write your description in your notebook. Be sure to include some history, a physical description, and your opinion.

SPEAKING

A Do you think it's a good idea or a bad idea to belong to a subculture? Make notes on why.

_____

_____

B IN PAIRS Discuss the questions. Explain your reasons. Use the Confident Communicator box to help you.

1 Do you think it's a good or a bad idea to belong to a subculture?
2 What are the advantages and the disadvantages?

CONFIDENT COMMUNICATOR
KEEP TALKING

To add a further point, say:
Also …
In addition to that, …
Not only that, but … also …
You can express your personality in a subculture. Not only that, but you can also meet people.

Language and Life

Media Literacy – Reaching a Target Group

A 12.05 **Read the article. Summarize how advertisers reach a particular target group. Write one sentence for each step in the process.**

REACHING A TARGET GROUP

Sometimes, a business has a product that it wants to sell to a certain group of people. For example, there is no point advertising a new car to people who don't drive. Governments, too, sometimes want to get information to a specific group. This might be information about children's health that they want to give to parents. In both cases, it would be a waste of money to inform everyone. It's better to aim your message at the people you want to reach. How do you do that?

First of all, it's important to clearly identify the group of people you want to reach. Is it parents? Is it teenagers? Is it homeowners? When you have a clear idea of your target group, then you can think about how to reach people in the group.

Second, you need to think about how to communicate with that group. Teenagers and young adults spend time on social networks. That might be the best way to reach them. It might not work so well for senior citizens or other groups.

Third, you need to express your message in the right way. With professional people, you may want to use serious language. With teenagers, you may want to use slang or informal language.

When you aim your message at a clear target group and use the right form of communication, your message is more effective.

1 ______________________________

2 ______________________________

3 ______________________________

B **IN PAIRS Read the situation and say in your own words what you need to do.**

You work in the marketing department of a restaurant chain. Sales are slow and they want to get more customers. Your boss has asked you to think about some target customers and to suggest ways of advertising to them.

C IN GROUPS Suggest what each group may want from a restaurant. Consider the elements from the list. Make notes below each picture.

- Type of food
- Type of tables and chairs
- Type of music
- Special services

families with young children

teenagers

professional people

senior citizens

D IN GROUPS Choose one group from C. Answer questions to design an advertisement to reach that group.

1 Which group is your target group? __________

2 What is the main thing they want from a restaurant? __________

3 What is the best way to communicate with your target group? __________

4 What kind of language will you use? __________

E IN GROUPS Design a poster, a TV ad, or an online post to communicate with your target group.

F IN GROUPS Share your ad with the class. Explain what you plan to do to reach your target group.

G Discuss the questions.

1 Whose ad do you think would reach the target group best? Why?

2 In what other situations or jobs do you need to create ads?

MAKE IT DIGITAL

Research online for creative ways to reach members of your social group or the social group of someone you know.

VOCABULARY review

SCORE: / 10

A Circle the correct option.

1 Networking is a good way of **coming** / **getting** to know people in your profession.
2 I like wearing **loose** / **tight** clothes because they're more comfortable when it's hot.
3 It's important to **do** / **make** time for your family when you are busy at work.
4 Do you **belong** / **join** to any clubs?
5 In my company, we have meetings every morning to **share** / **tell** ideas.
6 My mom doesn't often wear rings, earrings, or other **jewelry** / **make-up**.
7 I'm job **hunting** / **looking** right now, so I'm writing to ask companies about vacancies.
8 Do you have any **contacts** / **interns** who can help me get a job in that company?
9 I like to **purpose** / **chat** with other students after class. It helps me make new friends.
10 My dad has a mustache, but he doesn't have a **beard** / **belt**.

GRAMMAR review

SCORE: / 10

A Complete the sentences with reflexive pronouns.

1 After the lecture, I introduced ____________ to the speaker.
2 My brother hurt ____________ in an accident.
3 I would rather do things ____________ than have help from other people.
4 In an exam, make sure you give ____________ enough time to check your answers.
5 Amy tried to tell ____________ not to worry when she lost her job.

B Complete the sentences with the correct form of the verbs in parentheses.

1 How long ____________ Mrs. Anderson? (you/ know)
2 When you called, I ____________ something on Netflix. (watch)
3 If you ____________ a lot of money, what would you do with it? (find)
4 I ____________ Matt, but he sounds like an interesting guy. (meet)
5 Sara ____________ with her parents until she finds an apartment. (live)

16–20 correct: You can talk about networking and physical appearances. You can use reflexive pronouns.
0–15 correct: Look again at the Vocabulary and Grammar sections in the unit.

TOTAL SCORE: / 20

WHAT DO YOU KNOW NOW? Look back at page 117 and add the words you know now to the box.

FOLLOW A PRO BUSINESS

Take the quiz about business. Then go to **Follow A Pro** on page 138. Find the answers and learn more about business.

1 Which company was the first to be worth $1 trillion?
a Apple **b** Amazon **c** Microsoft

2 How many new businesses started up each month in the US during 2016?
a 50,000 **b** 250,000 **c** 550,000

3 Who is most comfortable with starting their own business?
a people over 35 **b** 25- to 35-year-olds **c** people under 25

4 According to a recent report, what is the best country to be an entrepreneur in?
a Japan **b** Germany **c** the US

UNIT 7

STUDY SKILLS

A **Look at two personal narratives. Which story is more interesting, in your opinion? Why?**

CREATIVITY

My First Day of College

I was a little nervous on my first day of college. I got lost on campus, and it took me half an hour to find my class. The professor seemed irritated that I arrived late, and I felt really stressed. I was lost and lonely because I didn't know anyone at the college. I didn't really need to worry because the other students were very nice. I'm still good friends with some of the people from my first day. The teachers here are very nice, too, and now I can find my way around the campus easily.

By Sebastian

My First Day of College

The college campus looked like a different planet. It felt light-years away from Earth and everything was unfamiliar. Finding my class on the first day was like going to the moon. It seemed like I was walking around in circles. I hunted for the classroom for half an hour before I landed there. I was a lonely alien in a crazy, crowded campus. Fortunately, the other life-forms on the planet were fun-loving and peaceful and became my new friends. After some time, everything became less strange.

By Elsa

B **Read Elsa's story again. What words does she choose to describe …**

1 the college campus? ____________________
2 how she arrived in class? ____________________
3 the other students? ____________________
4 how she felt? ____________________

C IN PAIRS **Read the definitions of a simile and a metaphor. Then write similes or metaphors to describe the things below.**

Simile: When you compare two things, saying that one is like another, e.g.: "The college campus looked like a different planet."
Metaphor: When you describe something as being something different (to show the similarities between the two things), e.g.: "I was a lonely alien."

1 falling in love ____________________
2 a stressful exam ____________________
3 a family party ____________________
4 a pet you love ____________________

D **Choose one of the ideas in C and write a paragraph. Use the simile or metaphor in your paragraph to make your writing interesting.**

My dog Laika is a hurricane. When she rushes into the room, there's noise, and nothing is safe ...

E THINKING SKILL—Brainstorm **In what ways are you creative? Do you enjoy expressing your feelings, solving problems, or inventing things? How can you use your creative gift in your life or work?**

MAKE IT HAPPEN

Keep a notebook of things you want to write about. Then choose one of the topics to write an essay about.

Answers to the quiz on page 76
1 c 2 b (It makes you more creative.) 3 b 4 b

UNIT 8

FOLLOW A PRO

A Read about a resort activities coordinator's job. Choose *True* or *False* below.

A RESORT ACTIVITIES COORDINATOR

Sergio Herrero is an activities coordinator at a large resort hotel in Costa Rica. He plans and directs sports and entertainment activities for children and adults, and he takes guests on nature walks along the beach. Sergio also coordinates the activities section on the hotel's website and helps manage the budget for his department.

Sergio is 24, and he has a degree in hotel management. He says that getting a management job right after graduation is very hard, and being an activities coordinator gives him some experience working for a large hotel. Sergio says the salary isn't great, but his expenses are low. He lives at the hotel and eats his meals there for free. Guests often tip the activities coordinators, and that's always nice!

Sergio says that an activities coordinator should have a college degree in a field like hotel management, sales and marketing, or sports management. It's important to speak English and one other language, especially at international resorts. And having the right personality is essential. Activities coordinators have to love people. They have to be friendly and enthusiastic, and they have to know how to play games and sports, and even sing or dance.

Sergio is enjoying his job and learning a lot about the hotel business. He says he especially likes meeting people from many different places around the world.

1 Entertaining guests is Sergio's only job responsibility. True / False
2 Sergio is working as an activities coordinator to get experience in hotel work. True / False
3 Being an activities coordinator has some benefits apart from the salary. True / False
4 You only have to speak one language to be an activities coordinator. True / False
5 Activities coordinators work with people of all ages. True / False
6 Sergio thinks that being an activities coordinator is a good way to enter the hotel business. True / False

B Discuss the questions as a class.

1 Is an activities coordinator's job important? Why or why not?
2 Have you ever seen an activities coordinator working? If so, tell the class about what you observed.
3 Would you like to be an activities coordinator? Why or why not?

VIDEO

WATCH THE VIDEO AND FOLLOW A RECREATION COORDINATOR.

C IN GROUPS Answer the questions.

1 What job is the video about? ______
2 What does the person do every day? ______
______
3 What is interesting about this job? ______
______
4 Does this person work long hours? ______
5 Is the person satisfied with the job? ______
6 Is there anything the person doesn't like? ______

D IN GROUPS Check your answers to the quiz on page 24 and discuss the questions.

1 Do you think you have the right qualifications to work as an activities coordinator?
2 What are some advantages and disadvantages of working as an activities coordinator?
3 What other leisure industry jobs can you think of?
4 What leisure industry jobs would be interesting to you?
5 What qualifications do you need to work in different jobs in the leisure industry?

Answers to the quiz on page 86
1 c 2 b 3 a, b, c, d, e

UNIT 9 STUDY SKILLS

A Read the conversation about a group of students working on a research project. Are the students using good problem-solving skills? Why or why not?

PROBLEM SOLVING

Carla: For our group assignment, we have to offer solutions to the lack of safe, affordable, and quick transportation to the college. It says here that we need to present three ideas for transportation, outlining the advantages and disadvantages of each idea.
Bobby: Right. Well, that's easy. Let's present an idea for a college taxi service. That's all we need!
Maggie: Yeah, it's safe, affordable, and it would be quick, too! Nice job. We're done!
Carla: Hold on! We're not finished yet. We need three different ideas, not just one.
Bobby: Oh, I forgot about that. So, we've already got a taxi service. How about self-driving taxis, too?
Carla: Yeah, OK. And maybe ride sharing, too?
Maggie: Yes. And why don't we find out how most students get to college in a typical week?
Bobby: Good idea. I'll ask my friends, OK? That'll be quick. That can be my part, and you can do all the other stuff.
Carla: No, we need to do more research than that! And we probably need to write a report. What do you think?
Maggie: Is that necessary? Can't we all just say what we want in a presentation?
Bobby: Yeah, that's probably the best plan.
Carla: Hmm … I'm not sure that's enough.
Maggie: Well, if you think we need a report, you can write it.

B Choose all the correct answers about the conversation in A.

The students aren't using good problem-solving skills because …

1. They haven't divided the work equally.
2. They aren't thinking about how to effectively research the problem.
3. They haven't considered several different solutions before deciding on three.
4. They haven't decided on a good way to research their topic.
5. They aren't sure if they have to write a report or just give the presentation.

C Number the steps in the problem-solving process in the correct order (1–4).

_____ Write down how you managed to solve the problem.
_____ Read the task carefully and make sure you understand it.
_____ Look at the problem in a few different ways. Think about many possible solutions.
_____ Decide what information you need to help you solve the problem.

D In your notebook, rewrite the conversation in A using your ideas and the problem-solving tips in C. Show good problem-solving skills.

E THINKING SKILL—Evaluate Employers look for employees who can help solve problems. What qualities does a good problem-solver have? Make a list.

Listens to everyone's opinion, ...

MAKE IT HAPPEN

Apply some of the problem-solving techniques you have learned to your own studies or work. Keep a journal about the process you used to solve a problem and decide what helped you reach a solution.

Answers to the quiz on page 96
1 a, b, c 2 a and c

UNIT 10

FOLLOW A PRO

A Read about a family physician's job. Answer the questions below.

A FAMILY PHYSICIAN

There are many different kinds of doctors. Grace Lincoln is a family physician.

"I always wanted to be a doctor from the time I was very young. I took a lot of science classes in high school and then majored in biology in college. I took anatomy, biology, and chemistry—all classes that are in a pre-med curriculum. After that, I went to medical school for four years and then had four more years of practical training before I got my present job. It's a long, hard road, but I can't imagine doing anything else.

"I use a lot of different skills every day. I need medical knowledge, of course, but I also need to be good with people. When my patients are ill or injured, they need the right treatment, but they also need to know that I understand how they feel. And I have to be ready for anything. My next patient might be an elderly person with a broken arm or a child with a fever. I love the feeling that I'm making a real difference in people's lives."

1 What kind of doctor is Grace? ______
2 When did Grace first want to be a doctor? ______
3 What was Grace's major as an undergraduate? ______
4 How many years of medical school and training did Grace complete before she got her job?
______
5 What does Grace like about her job? ______

B Discuss the questions as a class.

1 Would you like to be a doctor?
2 What do you think is the best part of being a doctor?

VIDEO

WATCH THE VIDEO AND FOLLOW A PHYSICAL THERAPIST.

C IN GROUPS Answer the questions.

1 What job is the video about? ______
2 What special skills or education does this person have? ______
______
3 Who does the person work with? ______
4 What are some of the good and bad things about the job? ______
______
5 Is the person's job hard? Why or why not? ______
______
6 Does this person need multiple languages to do this job? ______

D IN GROUPS Check your answers to the quiz on page 44 and discuss the questions.

1 Do you know anybody who works in health care?
2 How does someone become a doctor in your country?
3 What skills do you think a doctor needs?
4 Do men and women do the same jobs in health care in your country?
5 What area of health care would you most like to work in?

Answers to the quiz on page 106
1 c 2 a 3 c

STUDY SKILLS

A **Yadira is working on an essay for her science class. Read her notes and her paragraph. Has she used all of the facts in her writing? Underline the words she should replace with precise facts.**

USING PRECISE LANGUAGE IN ACADEMIC WRITING

Research Notes

- *70% of the Earth is covered in water*
- *less than 3% of the Earth's water is fresh water*
- *17% of people don't have clean drinking water*
- *cholera and dysentery are diseases caused by unclean water*
- *in developing countries, 80% of illnesses are caused by dirty drinking water*

How can we help more people have clean drinking water?

Most of the world's surface is covered by water, but not much of it is fresh. Many people have no access to clean water and this is really terrible. Clean water is very important for our health, and it is also important for keeping everything clean. Unclean drinking water causes some serious diseases, such as cholera and dysentery. These diseases stop people from working and cause economic problems. I think it's terrible that rich countries don't do more about this.

B **Read the tips on writing academic essays. Then rewrite the sentences with more precise language.**

- Use specific facts in your writing and be precise in your language. Look for statistics from reliable sources, such as books, journals, and trusted internet sites.
- Don't use generalizations (a lot of people say … , no one wants … , more people prefer …).
- Opinions are your personal beliefs. Don't give opinions in academic essays unless you also have facts to support your opinions.

1 Many students in my English class have studied English for more than a year.

____

2 Some students take a class in the morning, and some take a class at night.

____

3 I like taking a class at night because I don't like getting up early in the morning.

____

4 A face-to-face class is more fun than an online class. That's why a lot of students prefer to attend a class.

____

C **In your notebook, rewrite Yadira's paragraph in A using the tips for academic writing in B.**

D **THINKING SKILL—Apply** **Why is it important to know how to be precise in your writing? How could remembering these tips help you to be a better writer?**

MAKE IT HAPPEN

Choose a topic from your work or studies. Research facts about the topic and write a paragraph in academic style. Use data and precise language to explain the topic.

Answers to the quiz on page 116

1 b 2 b 3 a 4 b

UNIT 12

FOLLOW A PRO

A Read about an entrepreneur's job. Answer the questions below.

AN ENTREPRENEUR

I'm Juana Geller. I run my own ethical jewelry business. My company designs and sells jewelry made from eco-friendly materials. I started my business when I was a teenager. I wanted to buy and wear jewelry that was different from everyone else. I made necklaces from glass beads. My friends liked my designs, so I started making necklaces and selling them to friends and family.

After high school, I learned about eco-friendly jewelry. I attended workshops on materials that could be recycled. I worked very hard and did a lot of networking. I visited many stores and talked about my ideas. A few stores decided to sell my jewelry, and the managers gave me advice on running my business. Young people liked my jewelry and talked about it on social media. The business started to grow, and I decided to get a degree in business administration to help me run it better.

Today, my company employs 50 people, and our jewelry is in stores across the country. We also sell a lot online. To be successful as an entrepreneur, you need to be able to take risks and be confident while you do it. You won't get much sleep for the first few years, but with a little luck, it'll be worth it in the end!

1 What does Juana's company produce? ____________________
2 Why did Juana start her business? ____________________
3 How did Juana get started? ____________________
4 What qualifications does Juana have? ____________________
5 What does Juana say about being a successful entrepreneur? ____________________
____

B Discuss the questions as a class.

1 Is being self-employed a good idea? Why or why not?
2 Can you imagine being self-employed?

VIDEO

WATCH THE VIDEO AND FOLLOW AN ENTREPRENEUR.

C IN GROUPS Answer the questions.

1 What kind of job does this person do? ____________________
2 Where does this person work? ____________________
3 What are the person's working hours? ____________________
4 What special skills does this person need? ____________________
5 How did this person learn the skills for the job? ____________________
6 Why do you think this person likes his job? ____________________

D IN GROUPS Check your answers to the quiz on page 64 and discuss the questions.

1 Do you know people who have started their own businesses?
2 Would you like to start your own business? Why or why not?
3 What are the risks of starting your own business?
4 In what ways would English help in starting your own business?
5 What skills does an entrepreneur need?

Answers to the quiz on page 126
1 a 2 c 3 c 4 b (Japan was second and the US was third.)

Irregular Verbs

Infinitive	Simple past	Past participle
be	was/were	been
become	became	become
begin	began	begun
break	broke	broken
bring	brought	brought
build	built	built
buy	bought	bought
catch	caught	caught
choose	chose	chosen
come	came	come
cost	cost	cost
cut	cut	cut
do	did	done
draw	drew	drawn
drink	drank	drunk
drive	drove	driven
eat	ate	eaten
fall	fell	fallen
feed	fed	fed
feel	felt	felt
find	found	found
fly	flew	flown
get	got	gotten
give	gave	given
go	went	gone
grow	grew	grown
hang	hung	hung
have	had	had
hear	heard	heard
hit	hit	hit
hold	held	held
hurt	hurt	hurt
keep	kept	kept
know	knew	known
leave	left	left
let	let	let
lose	lost	lost
make	made	made
meet	met	met
pay	paid	paid
put	put	put
read	read	read
ride	rode	ridden
ring	rang	rung
rise	rose	risen
run	ran	run
say	said	said
see	saw	seen
sell	sold	sold
send	sent	sent
set	set	set
sing	sang	sung
sit	sat	sat
speak	spoke	spoken
stand	stood	stood
stick	stuck	stuck
take	took	taken
teach	taught	taught
tell	told	told
think	thought	thought
throw	threw	thrown
understand	understood	understood
wake	woke	woken
wear	wore	worn
win	won	won
write	wrote	written

Pronunciation Symbols

Vowels

ɪ	did
ɛ	bed
æ	bad
ʌ	cup
ʊ	book
ə	banana
i	feed
ɑ	father, box
ɔ	tall
u	student, food
ɝ	shirt, birthday
eɪ	date, table
aɪ	cry, eye
ɔɪ	boy
oʊ	comb, post
aʊ	about, how

Consonants

p	park, happy
b	back, hobby
t	tea
d	die
k	came, kitchen, quarter
g	game, go
f	face, photographer
v	vegetable
θ	thing, math
ð	then, that
s	city, summer
z	please, goes
ʃ	she, shop
ʒ	leisure
h	hot, who
tʃ	chicken, watch
dʒ	jacket, orange
m	men
n	sun, know
ŋ	sung, singer
w	week, white
r	rain, writer
l	light, long
j	yes, use, music

Grammar Review

A Match the questions (1–8) to the answers (a–h). Write the letter.

1 Do you like using social media? ______
2 How's it going? ______
3 Who do you live with? ______
4 When do you start work? ______
5 Is there a library in your town? ______
6 Can you run fast? ______
7 How much milk do we have? ______
8 Did he do his homework? ______

a We have half a liter.
b At 9 a.m.
c No, I can't!
d Good, thanks.
e No, there isn't.
f My parents and my brother.
g Yes, I do.
h Yes, he did.

B Complete the sentences with the phrases from the box.

has to | like to | need to | plan to | want to | would like to

1 Next year, I really ________________ travel the world.
2 ________________ you ________________ come with me?
3 I ________________ plan my trip before I go.
4 My passport ________________ be up to date.
5 I ________________ be away for about a year.
6 I ________________ travel. It's one of my favorite things.

C Complete simple past sentences using the verbs in parentheses.

1 Last weekend, I ________________ (celebrate) my birthday with family and friends.
2 We ________________ (go) to my favorite restaurant.
3 I ________________ (not have) a party at my home because my apartment is too small.
4 The meal ________________ (be) delicious, and we all really ________________ (enjoy) it.
5 We ________________ (not go) to a movie because it was so late when we finished dinner.
6 What ________________ (do) you do last weekend?

D Complete the conversation with the comparative form of the adjectives in parentheses.

Tim: Where do you want to eat this weekend? Do you want to go to the pizza place or the new restaurant?
Lara: Hmm, I don't know. The pizza place is **1** ________________ (cheap).
Tim: Yes, but I think the food at the new place is **2** ________________ (good). Their salads look good, too. I think you get **3** ________________ (healthy) food there.
Lara: You're probably right. I'm not sure about the staff at the new place. I think the waiters at the pizza place are **4** ________________ (friendly).
Tim: So many people are talking about the new restaurant, though! It's **5** ________________ (popular) than the pizza place.
Lara: Yes, but the pizza place is **6** ________________ (close), and it's raining.

E Rewrite the sentences correctly.

1 She can run really fastly. ______
2 She speaks English good. ______
3 Can you more slowly speak, please? ______
4 You need to do very carefully this. ______
5 He caught the ball easy. ______
6 He studied hardly for his exam. ______

F Read and choose the correct option.

I really love my hometown. **1 There are / There is** a lot of nice restaurants and **2 there are / there is** some small cafés, too. **3 There is / There are** a big library, and **4 there's / there are** a school. **5 There aren't / There isn't** too many stores, but there is a beautiful park. What about your town? **6 Are there / Is there** a lot of things to do?

G Complete the sentences with the present progressive form of the words in parentheses.

1 Rory ______ (take) a selfie.
2 Sula ______ (update) her profile.
3 Jan ______ (post) comments on a blog.
4 Manny and Luca ______ (send) texts to each other.
5 Mary's video ______ (go) viral.
6 Everyone ______ (look) at their screens.
7 They ______ (not speak) to each other.

H Read and choose the correct option.

Ava: Can I have **1 some / a** milk, please?
Will: Of course. **2 How much / How many** do you want?
Ava: I'd like a liter, please. Can I have **3 this / some** apples, too?
Will: Sure. **4 These / This** red ones?
Ava: No, **5 those / that** green ones, please.
Will: Here you go.
Ava: **6 How much / How many** is that, please?

UNIT 7 — present perfect with *already*, *just*, and *yet*

Function

We use *just* to show that an action has happened in the very recent past. We use *already* to show that an action has happened (sometimes sooner than expected). To show that an action is going to happen but hasn't happened, we use *yet* with the negative present perfect. To find out if an action has happened, we use the present perfect and *yet* in a question.

Form

already	*just*	*yet*
I've already started my new job. I've already applied for it.	I've just sent my resume. He's just called me. We've just met.	Have you met the boss yet? Have you thought about what you want to do yet? I haven't had an interview yet. They haven't contacted me yet.

A Unscramble and write the sentences for a conversation.

Luna: How's the job hunt going?
Henry: It's going well! **1** I've / PR firm / just / applied / for a job / with a
Luna: **2** seen / ! / I've / the perfect job / just / for you It's an internship at *Wave* magazine.
Henry: Oh! **3** that / already / I've / seen / job ad **4** I / sent / resume / haven't / my / yet
Luna: **5** interviews / yet / you / ? / had / have / any
Henry: **6** just / had / I've / an / email I have an interview with a news website on Friday.
Luna: That's great! Good luck.

1 ______________________________
2 ______________________________
3 ______________________________
4 ______________________________
5 ______________________________
6 ______________________________

B Choose the correct option.

1. She hasn't had any training **yet** / **already** because she's just started.
2. He's **already** / **yet** been promoted, and he's only worked there for a year!
3. I've **just** / **yet** gotten a raise! Let me buy the coffee this time.
4. Have you started working there **yet** / **just**?
5. They've **already** / **yet** gone home. They usually finish early on Fridays.
6. I've **just** / **yet** emailed her, so hopefully she'll reply soon.

UNIT 7 — present perfect and simple past

Function

We use the simple past to talk about an event that happened at a specific time in the past, to describe routines in the past, and to talk about events that happened at the same time or immediately after another event. We use present perfect to talk about an event that happened sooner than expected, to ask a question about whether something has happened, and to talk about an action that has been in progress for an amount of time, an action that happened in the very recent past, or an action that began in the past and will continue in the future.

Form

We form the simple past by adding *–ed* to the end of regular verbs. Some simple past forms are irregular. The present perfect is formed with the auxiliary *has/have* and the past participle.

	Present perfect	**Simple past**
Statements	I have (I've) lived here for five years. We have (we've) started a business together.	I lived here five years ago. We started a business together last year.
Questions and answers	Have you had breakfast? Yes, I have. / No, I haven't. Which countries have you visited? I've visited France and Egypt.	Did you have breakfast this morning? Yes, I did. / No, I didn't. Where did you visit last summer? I visited France.

A Read and choose the correct option.

Valerie: Hey, Zelia! I've just **1 had / have** a great idea. I'm going to start my own business.
Zelia: Wow! **2 Have you ever done / Did you ever do** anything like this before?
Valerie: No, **3 I worked / I've worked** at the same job since I graduated. I think it's time to do something different now.
Zelia: Cool! What are you going to do?
Valerie: Well, I've just **4 seen / saw** that there's a small building on Main Street for rent. I want to rent it and open my own restaurant.
Zelia: That's great! I've **5 thought / think** about starting a business, but I don't know if I could do it. You'll be great! Good luck.

B Complete the sentences with the present perfect or simple past form of the words in parentheses.

1 Hi, Sandra! ______________________________ (have) a good time last night?
2 Bob and I ______________________________ (work) at the same company for three years.
3 She ______________________________ (have) a job interview yesterday. I think it went well!
4 Last year, I ______________________________ (apply) for about 15 different jobs.
5 ______________________________ (see) my phone? I can't find it anywhere!

UNIT 8 — gerund phrases as subject and object

Function

A gerund is an *–ing* verb that functions as a noun. A gerund can be either the subject or the object of a sentence. We use a gerund after the verbs *prefer*, *enjoy*, *can't stand*, *like*, *love*, and *hate*.

Form

Gerund as subject	**Gerund as object**
Going outside on a cold and rainy day is fun. Spending time with you is always great! Painting is a really relaxing hobby.	Many people enjoy posting on social media. My friends love hanging out in the park. We always enjoy coming to visit you.

A Identify the errors and rewrite the sentences correctly.

Five Tips to Become More Creative

1 Face a blank page is always scary, but thinking up new ideas is great for your creativity.

____

____

2 If you hate brainstorm, why not try doing it with a friend? Two heads are better than one!

____

____

3 Do what you enjoy will help you feel more creative. Do you love be outdoors? Then get outside and enjoy some fresh air to help you think more clearly.

____

____

4 Be open to ideas is really important. If an idea doesn't work for you, then have another one.

____

____

5 Ask the right questions. Know what you want to do is probably the most important part of the creative process.

____

____

B Complete the sentences with a gerund phrase and a noun so that they are true for you.

1 *Doing* (do) *yoga* is a great way to help you relax and feel less stressed.
2 Lots of people enjoy ________ (go) ________ because they love nature.
3 ________ (join) ________ is a good way of meeting new people.
4 My family really likes ________ (spend) ________ together.
5 ________ (visit) ________ is a nice thing to do when you're in a new city.
6 My friends and I always enjoy ________ (have) ________ together.
7 My dad can't stand ________ (do) ________.

UNIT 8 — verb + gerund or infinitive

Function

Some verbs are followed by an infinitive (*to* + verb), while some verbs are followed by a gerund (verb + *–ing*). Some verbs (e.g., *like*) can be followed by either an infinitive or a gerund (this does not change the meaning).

Form

Love, like, hate, prefer **+ infinitive / *–ing* verb**	***Would like*** **+ infinitive**
I hate eating alone. We prefer to shop online. She likes eating out with friends.	He'd like to see her again. We'd like to stay a little longer. I'd like to thank you for your help.
Would prefer **+ infinitive**	***Would rather*** **+ base verb**
I'd prefer to travel by plane. She'd prefer to do it herself.	I'd rather see an action film. They'd rather know the truth.

A Read and choose the correct option.

Elena: Hey, it's the long weekend! Susie's rented a house at the beach, and she's invited us! Do you want to go?

Tom: Hmm, I don't know. Susie likes really action-packed vacations, and you know I prefer **1 chill out / to chill out**.

Elena: I know you do! I like relaxing, too, but I hate **2 to waste / waste** a holiday weekend doing nothing.

Tom: Well, we can compromise. Would you like **3 to go / going** and spend the day with Susie?

Elena: Hmm, it's a long drive. I'd prefer **4 staying / to stay** overnight. The house looks beautiful! Here's a picture.

Tom: Well, it does look nice. OK, let's go and stay overnight. I'd rather **5 stay / to stay** Friday night than Saturday night, if that's OK. There's a football game on TV Saturday that I would really like **6 seeing / to see**.

UNIT 9 — future forms: *will, going to,* present progressive, and simple present

Function

We use *will* or *going to* when we make predictions about the future. To talk about arrangements, we use present progressive, and to talk about intentions, we use *going to*. To talk about future events that are scheduled to happen, we use the simple present.

Form

will			
Affirmative			**Questions**
I You He/She It We They	will/'ll	see you later. be back. do really well. all work out. eat here again. make friends easily.	Will you try harder next time? Will we go shopping? **Negative** She won't make that mistake again. It won't rain—the sky is blue.

going to	**Present progressive**	**Simple present**
I'm going to study law. It's not going to rain. She's not going to live there. Are you going to travel?	You're having lunch. He's seeing her tomorrow. We're not getting up early. Is he visiting her tomorrow?	School starts at 9 a.m. We leave at 3 a.m. The train doesn't leave until tomorrow morning. When does the plane take off?

A Complete the conversations with words and phrases from the box.

are thinking does going to I'm moving we're meeting we'll won't you'll

1 **Nicanor:** I'm tired of sharing an apartment. I'm ______________ start looking for a place of my own.
Luis: That's a good idea. Places are expensive, though. Do you think ______________ find something?
2 **Ellie:** We ______________ find an apartment in this neighborhood. Everything's so expensive!
Leah: Don't be so pessimistic! ______________ find something.
3 **Aria:** Have you heard the news? ______________ into a new apartment!
Pedro: Congratulations! When ______________ your lease start?
4 **Adara:** Mariam and I ______________ about sharing an apartment.
Batul: That sounds like a good idea!
Adara: ______________ later today to talk about it.

UNIT 9 — future possibility and certainty (*may, might, could, will, won't, probably, definitely*)

Function

We use *may*, *might*, and *could* to talk about things that are possible in the future. We use *probably* when we are almost sure about the future. We use *definitely* when we are very sure about the future.

Form

Future possibility	Future probability
I might go there. She may study there. They could move to a new house.	I'll probably come to the party.
Future certainty	**Negative future possibility**
I'll definitely email her.	He may not be happy. She might not like it.
Question form	**Short answers**
Do you think you might …? Do you think you'll …?	Yes, I might. / No, I might not. Yes, I definitely/probably will.

A Read and choose the correct option.

Cameron: What are your plans for next year? Do you think you **1 might / definitely** move out of your parents' house?

Janet: Yeah, I might. I'm not sure, though. I'm in my final year of college, so I'll **2 might / probably** have to study a lot more. I **3 probably / might** have to give up my part-time job, so I'll **4 probably / might not** have less money.

Cameron: Yeah, the final year is tough, believe me! You'll **5 may / definitely** have to study more. It **6 may / probably** be a good idea to stay with your parents for another year.

Janet: Why do you think that?

Cameron: Well, it's not always easy sharing an apartment. You **7 might / definitely** not get along with your roommates.

Janet: Yeah, I suppose you're right! Oh, well, Mom and Dad **8 probably / could** won't be upset if I hang around for another year.

B Unscramble and write the sentences.

1 an / rent / next / I'll / definitely / apartment / year / .

____

2 probably / share / we'll / bills / the / .

____

3 you / next / think / do / live / you'll / alone / year / ?

____

4 she / study / in / different / a / may / country / .

____

5 might / I / not / go / the / movies / to / .

____

6 our / apartment / balcony / have / new / won't / probably / a / .

____

7 definitely / they'll / be / tomorrow / there / .

____

UNIT 10 — zero and first conditional

Function

The zero conditional expresses general facts and scientific truths. The first conditional expresses real possibilities in the present or future. When the *if* clause is at the beginning of the sentence, it should be followed by a comma.

Form

Zero conditional	
***if* clause (*if* + present tense)**	**Result clause (present tense)**
If you eat well, If a person exercises every day,	you feel well. he or she feels more energetic.

First conditional	
***if* clause (*if* + present tense)**	**Result clause (will + base verb)**
If you drink more water, If she takes some time to relax,	your skin will look clearer. she'll feel better.

A Use the prompts in parentheses to complete the conversation.

Selena: I don't feel good. If I stand up quickly, **1** ______________ (feel / dizzy).

Marco: You're working too hard. **2** ______________ (work at computer) for hours without taking a break, you'll feel pretty terrible afterward.

Selena: You're right. I need to make some lifestyle changes.

Marco: Yeah, I think you do. You're working too hard, and you're not eating well. **3** ______________ (make bad choices), you won't feel so good.

Selena: True! I don't have time to eat healthy meals.

Marco: It doesn't need to take a lot of time. If you drink more water, **4** ______________ (stop / get headaches), for example. Drinking water doesn't take too much time, does it?

Selena: I guess not. And I suppose if I eat less sugar, **5** ______________ (have / more energy)—isn't that what they say?

Marco: Yeah. **6** ______________ (make / small changes), it's easier to keep going with them. Good luck!

UNIT 10 — second conditional

Function

We use the second conditional to talk about hypothetical or impossible situations in the present or future.

Form

***if* clause (*if* + past tense)**	**Result clause (*would, could, might* + base verb)**
If I lost my credit card, If I found a lost puppy, If she had a million dollars, If I was talented at music,	I would / I'd call the bank. I could take it home. she might start her own business. I'd learn to play the flute.
If I got lost in New York, If he told me his biggest secret,	I wouldn't panic. I wouldn't tell anyone.

A Read and choose the correct option.

What would I do if I **1 won / win** a million dollars? Well, first of all, **2 I call / I'd call** all my friends, and **3 I'll / I'd** ask them to come to my house. Then **4 I'd / I'll** have a big party. If I was rich, **5 I might want / I might wanting** some new clothes, so my friends and I **6 would go / go** shopping at our favorite stores. We'd **7 buy / bought** some elegant clothes, and then we'd go to the best restaurant in town. **8 If / When** we decided to eat at the best restaurant in town, we'd want to travel in style, so I think **9 I'd / I'll** hire a limousine for the occasion.

B Identify the mistakes and rewrite the sentences correctly.

1 If you doing more exercise, you'd feel better.

______

2 If it snowed tomorrow, I go skiing.

______

3 If I lived near the beach, I learn to surf.

______

4 If they asked you to work for them, do you say yes?

______

5 What would you do if you'll miss the bus?

______

6 If you spoke a foreign language, you can get a really good job.

______

7 If we have a yard, we'd have a barbecue every night in the summer.

______

UNIT 11 — simple present passive

Function

We use the present passive to focus on the thing that receives the action, when we don't know who or what does something, when it's obvious or unimportant who or what does something.

Form

Affirmative		Negative	
Auxiliary *be* in simple present	**+ past participle of the verb**	**Auxiliary *be* in simple present + not**	**+ past participle of the verb**
Volkswagen cars are Indian films are Oranges are	made in Germany. shot in Bollywood. grown here.	Tiramisu isn't Grapes aren't	made from oranges. produced in Iceland.

A Complete the steps using the present passive.

How Glass Is Recycled

1 Glass / empty *The glass is emptied.*
2 Glass bottle / take / recycling center ______
3 Glass / sort / by color ______
4 Glass / crush and melt ______
5 Glass / make / into new products ______
6 New product / sell / stores ______
7 Glass / empty / take / recycling center ______

B Identify the mistakes and rewrite the sentences correctly.

1 Our room is be cleaned at the moment. ______
2 English is speaked all over the world. ______
3 Credit cards are accepting here. ______
4 About 100,000 people are employ by this company. ______
5 His invention is now sell in 45 different countries. ______
6 Her name is knowing throughout the country. ______

UNIT 11 — simple past passive

Function

We use the simple past passive to focus on the thing that received the action, when we don't know who or what did something, when it's obvious or unimportant who or what did something.

Form

Affirmative		Negative	
Auxiliary *was/were* in simple past	**+ past participle of the verb**	**Auxiliary *was/were* in simple past + not**	**+ past participle of the verb**
The biro pen was	invented by a Hungarian, Laszlo Biro.	I wasn't	invited to the party.
We were given	free coffee.	We weren't seen	by a doctor.

A Complete the text using the simple past passive forms of the verbs in parentheses.

I **1** __________ (give) a really cool birthday present last Christmas—grass flip-flops! When you wear them, you feel like you're walking on grass. Grass flip-flops **2** __________ (invent) by an Australian man who loved the feeling of grass under his feet!

My best-ever present **3** __________ (give) to me by my best friend, Anna. It's a beautiful picture of a Scottish landscape, and it's special because it **4** __________ (take) by her.

On my last birthday, I got a pair of socks. They **5** __________ (knit) by my aunt, and they **6** __________ (make of) hard, scratchy wool. I didn't like them very much!

UNIT 12 — reflexive pronouns

Function

We use reflexive pronouns when the subject and the object of the sentence are the same. We can also use reflexive pronouns to mean "without help from another person."

Form

Subject pronoun	Reflexive pronoun	Example
I	myself	I taught myself to dance.
You	yourself	Help yourself to food!
He	himself	He made himself a sandwich.
She	herself	She bought herself a coat.
It	itself	It switched itself off.
We	ourselves	We consider ourselves lucky.
You	yourselves	Did you build this yourselves?
They	themselves	They found themselves homeless.

A Match the halves to make sentences.

1 I was feeling cold, so I bought ____
2 It was a great feeling to find ____
3 You can teach ____
4 He doesn't see ____
5 Clara and Miguel found ____
6 Make yourself ____

a myself a hot drink.
b at home!
c themselves in a large, bright classroom.
d himself as an optimistic person.
e yourself just about anything nowadays.
f myself part of a big, friendly group.

B Complete the conversation with the words from the box.

do it myself	herself	motivate myself	myself	ourselves	see myself	yourself

Suki: I taught **1** ________________ to read Chinese when I was 10.

Malik: Wow—you taught **2** ________________? You must be really motivated.

Suki: Yeah, I suppose I do **3** ________________ as a motivated person.

Malik: That's impressive. I can never **4** ________________ to do things like that!

Suki: Well, I really wanted to go to China, and there were no language classes in my area, so I just had to **5** ________________.

Malik: That reminds me of my sister. She really wanted to learn ballet, but there were no classes in our area. She spent hours watching YouTube videos and she taught **6** ________________!

Suki: Wow! That's really cool! Hey, you're coming on the study trip to Germany next year, aren't you? Why don't we teach **7** ________________ German? Maybe you'd feel more motivated if we learned together.

Malik: Sure!

UNIT 12 — tense review

Function and form

Use	Example
We use the simple present to talk about a present state or habit. We also use the simple present to talk about a future scheduled event.	I share an apartment with some friends. The train leaves at three in the afternoon.
We use the present progressive to talk about an action in progress now. We also use the present progressive to talk about a future arrangement.	I'm waiting for my taxi to get here. We're meeting each other this afternoon.
We use the simple past to talk about a past state or habit.	I loved that TV show when I was younger!
We use the past progressive to talk about an action in progress at a past moment.	It was snowing when we were at the shops.
We use the present perfect to talk about a situation that started in the past and continues to the present moment.	She's been my teacher for three years now.
We use the second conditional to talk about hypothetical situations.	If I had a car, I'd give you a lift.

A Read and choose the correct option.

1 Have / **Did** you ever felt shy on your first day of a new job? When I started my new job, **2 I** / **I've** felt really nervous because I didn't know anyone. Then one day, when I **3 was leaving** / **left** the office, one of my colleagues asked me if I wanted to join the company's tennis club. I said, **4** "**I've** / **I** never played tennis before," but my colleague said it didn't matter. I decided to go along. Two years later, I **5 am knowing** / **know** a lot of people, and I don't feel shy anymore. In fact, next year **6 I'm playing** / **play** in a tennis tournament with some workers from another company! If I wasn't part of the tennis club, I think I **7 might not know** / **maybe don't know** so many people.

Unit 7

Track 01

How Career-Ready Are You?

Have you started your career yet? If you have just started working, you are probably very happy and are learning a lot about your job. However, if you have already worked for a while, you are probably thinking about how to improve your career options. If you haven't started working yet, you are probably thinking about what kind of career you want. It is always a good idea to think about the next step in your working life.

First, it is important to understand that being career-ready refers to more than training and knowledge about a job or a career. It refers to a combination of knowledge, skills, and personal characteristics.

Knowledge includes the academic or technical information that you need for a career area or a specific job, but it also includes other types of knowledge. For example, you may need general math skills or a good level of English.

Skills include specific technical skills, but they also include skills like using your time well, the ability to communicate, and working in a team. One of the most important skills today is the ability to solve problems.

Finally, you need to understand what personal characteristics and personality types are ideal for different jobs and careers. Some people with excellent academic qualifications are unhappy in their careers because their jobs don't really match their personalities.

It doesn't matter if you have just graduated from high school or college, haven't graduated yet, or already have a job; you should take some time to think about your future. How career-ready are you?

Track 02

yard	year	yellow	yes
yesterday	yet		
you	young	jacket	jet
job	John		
juice	Julie	jump	just

Track 03

1 Julie bought a yellow jacket yesterday.
2 Yes, you can have some juice.
3 Have you met John yet?
4 James has just started a new job in New York.

Track 04

Host: Welcome to *Our Community*. I'm interviewing Carmen Vega, a very successful entrepreneur in our community. Carmen is the owner of That's Cool!, the most popular ice cream shop in town. Carmen, how long has the shop been in business?

Carmen: I've been in business for five years now. When I started, I hired one employee. I made the ice cream and she served the customers.

Host: That's Cool! is now the number one ice cream shop in the community. Why have you been so successful?

Carmen: That's simple. We have great ice cream!

Host: The ice cream is fantastic, but for a business to succeed, it also needs good management. Do you have a degree in business?

Carmen: No, I don't. I started college, majoring in architecture, but I didn't graduate.

Host: What happened?

Carmen: Well, one summer I was bored, so I took a class to learn how to make ice cream. I loved it! I made about twenty kinds of ice cream that summer.

Host: Is that when you started the business?

Carmen: No. I went back to college in the fall, but I really wasn't very interested in it. Then my sister said, "Why don't you try to sell your ice cream?" I thought it was an excellent idea, so when school was out in the spring, I opened the ice cream shop. I never went back to college.

Host: Do you like owning your own business?

Carmen: I love it! I didn't have to apply for a job, try to get a raise or a promotion, or climb the corporate ladder.

Host: Well, you've had an interesting career path. How many ice cream flavors have you invented so far?

Carmen: I'm not sure, but more than twenty, I think. I've just created a new flavor called Orange Chill. It has green chilies and oranges.

Host: Oh, wow! Have you started selling it yet?

Carmen: Yes, we have. We started selling it last week, and we've already sold out!

Host: Carmen, thanks for talking to me, and congratulations on your success.

Carmen: Thank you.

Track 05

Nick: Good morning. I'm your host, Nick Walker, and the topic of our talk today is getting a job in the 21st century. Please welcome Barbara Nelson, from Job Search Consultants. Barbara, can you explain what 21st century employability skills are?

Barbara: Yes, of course. In the past, employers usually looked at two things, college degrees and work experience, but that has changed. Now employers want to hire people who also have other skills, and sometimes those skills are more important.

Nick: That's interesting. Is it possible that someone who is, for example, very organized, creative, and motivated could get a better job than someone with a degree from a good university?

Barbara: Definitely. Let me give you an example. I had two good candidates for a job as finance manager for a big company. I'll call them Joe and James. Joe had a master's degree in finance from a very good university. James didn't have a master's, and he went to an average university.

Nick: Let me guess. James got the job.

Barbara: Yes, he did. Joe had good technical knowledge, but a manager has to work with people, and James had better interpersonal skills. He showed that he was flexible and enjoyed working in a team. He was also curious, and he asked a lot of interesting questions about the bank and its employees. Finally, he seemed more motivated to learn new things and try creative ways to solve problems.

Nick: So if you're flexible, motivated, curious, and creative, you can sometimes stand out more than someone with only excellent academic qualifications or a lot of work experience.

Barbara: That's right. Of course, it's best to have excellent skills and great qualifications.

Nick: Sure. Barbara, thank you for this important information.

Barbara: You're welcome, Nick.

Track 06

Turn Skills into Sales

Have you ever thought about starting your own business? These days, more and more young people are doing just that. There are many types of businesses that are not very expensive to start. Often you just need a computer, but you also need to be motivated and patient because starting a business takes a lot of time and hard work. There are several areas that offer good business opportunities for young people.

- If you are creative, make handmade items: clothes, jewelry, soap, hand-painted T-shirts, origami designs, or greeting cards.
- Are you good at photography? Take pictures and sell them to online stock photo companies. Take photos or make videos of weddings, family reunions, or community events. Start a pet portrait business.
- Can you cook? Make cookies or cupcakes to sell to friends, at community events, or online.
- Do you love animals? Think about dog walking or pet sitting. You can also make different flavors of dog treats.
- If you have good computer skills, there are many possibilities for making money. Start a device setup service to help people get started with new computers, tablets, phones, or any other device. Become a tech tutor to teach children or older people how to use computers.
- Do you like public speaking, writing, or performing? If you have interesting things to say, you can start a blog or a vlog and get money from advertisers. Maybe you

can become a video personality, or create videos to teach people how to do things.

- Finally, one of the easiest ways to make money is to sell things online. Sell items that your family doesn't use anymore, and buy things online or at garage sales and resell them.

Unit 8

Track 01

Kids + Adults = Kidults

Adults like having toys—no, not boats, sports equipment, or expensive audio equipment, but actual children's toys. They are making things with building blocks, coloring in coloring books, making art with 3D pens, and doing difficult puzzles; they are bouncing inside enormous plastic balls and flying kites. There is a new term for adults who love playing like children: *kidults*.

Why is this happening? Experts think that in part it is because people, especially millennials, want an escape from the complications of the modern world. Acting like a child is a way to return to a simpler time, but there is another reason for this trend. Doing kids' activities is fun! Why shouldn't adults enjoy doing things like flying kites or coloring?

People over 50 also spend time doing children's activities. Many grandparents are very healthy and active, and they love playing with their grandchildren. Seniors are playing board games, doing arts and crafts, and participating in other activities that kids love.

Being an adult doesn't mean that you have to be serious all the time or pay a lot of money for entertainment. Are you creative? Try building a model or making a sculpture with clay. Maybe you love being active, but you can't stand playing competitive sports. Try jumping rope or flying a kite. Find your inner child and enjoy being a kidult!

Track 02

Marta: Yay, today's Friday!
Ken: Yeah! What do you guys want to do this weekend? Kate?
Kate: I want to do something different. We always do the same stuff – go to a movie or hang out at somebody's house. Doing the same things all the time is boring!
Stefan: Kate's right. Why don't we actually make a plan for the whole weekend?
Marta: Great idea! OK, what do we all like doing? I love going out to hear live music. I'd like to do that Saturday night.
Ken: Sure. Live music is a good idea.
Stefan: Cool. I'll find out who's playing at the clubs. What about during the day?
Kate: I'd like to do something creative. There are one-day classes in arts and crafts at the community center. You can learn how to make something, like candles or simple jewelry.
Ken: I don't know. I'd rather do a physical activity. I don't really like doing arts and crafts.
Marta: I know! Let's go paddle boarding on the river.
Ken: Paddle boarding is an awesome idea! Stefan and Kate? What do you guys think?
Stefan: Sure. Let's go for it. I prefer doing physical activities, too.
Kate: Fine with me. So Saturday is paddle boarding and then live music in the evening. What about Sunday?
Stefan: Why don't we have a picnic? We can go for a drive and look for a nice place to spend the morning.
Ken: OK, but I would prefer to do it later in the day. I hate getting up early on Sunday!
Kate: That sounds good. I'd prefer to go later, too.
Stefan: So do we have a plan, or would you rather think of some other options?
Marta: I'm fine with this plan.
Ken: Me, too.
Kate: That sounds good. It will be fun and different.

Track 03

Omar: Would you like to go to the new museum tomorrow?
Jamal: That sounds great. We should go early, when there are fewer people.
Omar: Actually, I would rather go in the afternoon. Is that OK?
Jamal: That's fine. Could you pick me up?
Omar: Sure.

Track 04

Professor: Good morning. I have a question for you. How often do you do nothing, and how do you feel when you are doing nothing?
Noah: I get bored. I would rather be busy all the time.
Tasha: Yeah, I agree. If I sit around and do nothing, I feel guilty. I prefer to finish everything I have to do.
Paul: Wow, I totally disagree. I think doing nothing helps you relax, so when you start working or studying, you feel rested. I often take a break to sit in the park or just lie on the sofa.
Magda: I agree about relaxing, but I'd rather watch a movie or read a book. To me, that's doing nothing. It makes me nervous to do absolutely nothing.
Professor: OK, how many think that things like reading or checking your social media are doing nothing? OK, about half the class. How many think that doing nothing is bad? More than half.
Paul: So, Professor Nelson, is it bad to do nothing?
Professor: Not necessarily. In fact, a lot of psychologists say that doing nothing is healthy. Being busy all the time is stressful, and it's hard to work or study well when you're stressed. Also, doing nothing helps you be more creative, and that helps you solve problems.
Magda: So, Professor Nelson, can our homework be to do nothing?
Professor: Yes, it can! Actually, your homework for next class is to take some time to do nothing, at least one hour, and I mean absolutely nothing. No social media, TV, reading, or whatever. Just do nothing. After one hour, write down what you were thinking and feeling while you were doing nothing. Was it a positive or a negative experience?

Track 05

Mindfulness for Mental Relaxation

Study, work, family, friends, pets, social media … We feel tired and stressed because we can't do everything. The effects of this are that we are less efficient, less creative, and less happy. We all try to do leisure activities like playing sports or watching movies, but what about leisure time for the mind?

In recent years, many people have started to practice *mindfulness*. Being mindful means that you are paying attention to what you are doing at the moment, to your feelings, and to the things that are happening around you. You are not thinking about things that have already happened or worrying about what is going to happen. For example, if you notice how the sun feels on your face, or how your clean clothes smell, you are being mindful.

There are some simple things that you can do to practice mindfulness. Do you like walking? Go for a walk, but don't think about walking fast or going a certain distance. Walk slowly. Think about how your body feels. Stop and look at trees or flowers. Stop and close your eyes. What do you hear, feel, or smell? Would you rather do something creative? Paint something or do a craft. Don't worry if it isn't good. Think about the process. How does the paintbrush feel in your hand? What does each color make you think of? Giving your brain time to relax can help you feel less stressed and more rested. The result is more creativity and better problem solving.

Unit 9

Track 01

Housing Solutions

In many areas, people can't afford to buy or rent a place to live. It's a problem that will become worse in the future. Some cities have found interesting solutions.

One example is half-houses in Chile. An earthquake hit the town of Constitución in 2010 and destroyed about 80% of the buildings. The local government hired an architecture firm to provide low-cost houses. They built houses that are only half-finished. The owners finish the house when they have the money. It means that each family can decide what they need: a garage, another bedroom, a hall, a balcony. One resident says: "We're going to build another bedroom and bathroom in two years. We can add our personal style."

Another solution is micro-units, like those at Carmel Place in New York City. These are very small apartments, around 28 square meters. They are too small for a family, but perfect for single young professionals. Each one-room apartment has the usual appliances—a stove, a refrigerator, and a microwave—and there's a room in another part of the building for washing clothes. The smart use of special furniture means the room can become a bedroom, kitchen, office, or living room. The desk becomes a dining table and the couch becomes a bed. The coffee table folds down and goes under the bed at night. A young resident says: "I'm having a friend over for dinner tonight. I just turn the bed into a couch, the desk into a table, and we're good to go!"

Track 02

Ethan: We graduate this summer, Ashley. I'm going to start apartment hunting. Where do you think you might live next year?

Ashley: Oh, I don't know. I want a job in finance, so maybe I'll live in an apartment near the financial district. If I don't find a job, I won't be able to afford it. And I might still be at home with my mom and dad. And that's fine. I like living with them.

Ethan: You could live with a friend. My brother and a couple of friends rent an apartment together. They have their own bedrooms and they share a living room, kitchen, and bathroom. They share the bills and the chores.

Ashley: I'd like to have roommates, but renting is so expensive. I probably won't be able to afford that.

Ethan: You may find something cheap outside the city. But then you have the problem of traveling into the city every day for work.

Ashley: What about you?

Ethan: I can't wait to have my own place. If I find a good job, I might rent a studio apartment downtown. I'd like to be downtown because I'd be close to all the restaurants and places to go.

Ashley: That sounds great, but you might get lonely living alone. You should think about renting a room in a house. And won't you miss living with your family?

Ethan: I will definitely miss them! But they could come and see me. I think I might ask my brother what it's like. Maybe I could live with him!

Ashley: Good idea!

Track 03

1	/aʊ/ like *house*: found sound	allow now	
2	/oʊ/ like *go*: own	below phone	know

Track 04

Hello, everyone. Today, I want to talk about the future of our homes. We're going to see many changes in our homes, but I'd like to focus on energy. The appliances in our houses, such as air conditioners and heaters, use a lot of energy. In the future, more and more people are going to be using renewable energy such as wind power, wave power, and solar power.

Here's a diagram explaining how solar power works. On the roof of the house, we have solar panels. These receive sunlight on sunny days. The light falls on special materials, which create electricity. This electricity is direct current, or DC. That goes to the inverter from the solar panels. The inverter changes the DC into AC, or alternating current. It then sends the electricity to the appliances in the house. Things like your kitchen stove, dishwasher, and washing machine need AC to work.

Sometimes, the system creates a lot of energy. In that case, the electrical grid takes the power that the house doesn't need. That way, other houses can use the electricity. And on days when there is no sun, the grid provides the house with power.

In the future, we might see solar windows on buildings. We could also see solar clothes or solar sunglasses. You wear them and they work like solar panels, creating energy to power your devices.

Track 05

Neighborhood Development

Neighborhoods are changing all the time. That means someone has to make decisions about these changes. It might be urban planners or members of local government. They often have to decide between different plans for a neighborhood. They may have to think about costs, housing, and the needs of local people. How do they make their decisions?

One tool to help planners make a decision is a decision matrix. In a decision matrix, they list the important results they want for the neighborhood. For example, local people may want more houses, less traffic, or more parks. Planners develop several plans to get these results. They then score each plan against each result: –2 for a very negative effect, –1 for a negative effect, 0 for no effect, +1 for a positive effect, and +2 for a very positive effect. The plan with the highest total score is the one to choose.

People can use a decision matrix to help with all kinds of decisions, from large business decisions to personal decisions like making a budget or planning a vacation.

Unit 10

Track 01

3 Ways to Power Up Your Brain!

How can you help your brain to work better? Here is some advice from the experts.

- Get healthy

One way to help your brain is to get healthy by exercising more and eating better. In one study, people had a better memory after six weeks of physical training. Some studies found that if you exercise for 10 minutes before thinking about a problem, it improves your problem-solving and decision-making skills. Your diet is also important. Vitamins and minerals from food—like fish, vegetables, and nuts—help keep your brain healthy.

- Sleep better

Sleep isn't just rest for the body. It also rests your brain. During sleep, your brain organizes your experiences, often through dreams. When you are learning new skills, you actually get better at them while you sleep! Sleep helps you think clearly while you're awake. Most people who sleep only four to six hours in one night don't think clearly the next day.

- Keep learning

Your brain can change, something known as neuroplasticity. If you challenge your brain, it will develop more connections between its neurons. One thing you can do to challenge your brain is to learn a new skill, such as a new language or a musical instrument. Some people enjoy brain training—online sites and apps that use puzzles or other tasks to exercise your brain. Many of these sites and apps don't have much effect on the brain, and they certainly won't make you more intelligent. However, psychologists have created some types of puzzles that make your brain work faster. Doing these tasks makes some people feel sharper in their everyday lives.

Track 02

Dan: Hello, I'm Dan Foster. This week, our guest is Madison Gray. Madison is a nurse, and she's going to be talking to me about being ready for accidents. Madison, what's the first thing we should know about accidents?

Madison: The most important thing is to have some basic training in first aid for common accidents. If you saw someone trip and fall while walking on the sidewalk, what would you do?

Dan: I guess I would help the person up.

Madison: That's not a good idea. If the person was injured, you could make the injury worse. First, I would see if he or she was awake. If the answer was yes, I would ask the person how he or she felt. I would check for injuries like a broken wrist or a sprained ankle. Then I might help the person sit up, and if that was OK, I'd help the person stand.

Dan: And what if the person wasn't awake?

Madison: Then I would see if he or she was breathing. If not, I'd do CPR and call an ambulance. If the person was breathing, I would try to make him or her comfortable. Then I would call an ambulance.

Dan: OK. What about something like a broken arm?

Madison: First, I would check for any cuts. It's important to stop any bleeding first because you can lose a lot of blood very quickly. If there were any cuts, I would press on them with a clean cloth. Then I would find a way to keep the arm from moving. If I could, I would put ice on the arm for the pain. Finally, I would call an ambulance.

Dan: We'll be back with more from Madison after these messages.

Track 03

If I had a cough, I would buy some medicine.

Track 04

1 If I broke my leg, I would call an ambulance.
2 If I had a rash, I'd search for information online.
3 If I sprained my ankle, I'd ask a friend for help.

Track 05

Aiden: Hi, Emily!
Emily: Hi, Aiden. Hey, you look like you're going to go running. I didn't know you were a fitness fanatic!
Aiden: I wasn't a fitness fanatic. I used to just sit in front of the TV when I got home from work, but I really needed to change that.
Emily: So you're running now?
Aiden: Well, yeah. There's a new program, called Couch to 5K. It's for people who want to get fit but don't know where to start. They take you from lying on the couch to running five kilometers in just nine weeks.
Emily: Sounds interesting! What did you have to do to get ready to run that much?
Aiden: Before I got started, I went to my doctor for a check-up. He said I was good to go and could get started any time.
Emily: So you just started running?
Aiden: Not exactly. In the first week of the program, I did three runs. On each run, I ran for one minute and then walked for a minute and a half. And each week, the program says to run just a little longer, and then walk. I'm only on Week 5, but after nine weeks, I'll run for 30 minutes and do five kilometers.
Emily: That sounds like a good way to get fit. I think even I could do that! What else do you have to do?
Aiden: You can get apps to help you improve your diet. You enter what food you eat and it tells you about the calories, the protein, that kind of thing. If you eat the right things, it means you won't get tired when you're exercising.
Emily: I might try it. Enjoy your run, and I'll call you later. You can tell me more about it.
Aiden: OK. See you later.

Track 06

Public Health

Many countries face serious public health problems. One example is obesity. According to the Organisation for Economic Co-operation and Development, one in two adults and nearly one in six children in its member countries are overweight or obese. That puts pressure on health services. Some countries are looking at ways of improving public health.

One way is to encourage people to eat better. Some countries, such as the United States and the United Kingdom, have five-a-day campaigns. They tell people that they should eat five portions of fruit or vegetables each day. Many countries have laws about labels on food. Producers have to show the amount of fat, protein, and carbohydrates in each food. Some countries have a "traffic light" system. Green means the food has a small amount of fat, sugar, and salt. Yellow means the food has a medium amount. Red means there's a high amount of fat, sugar, or salt. The labels help people make better choices.

Public health departments are always looking for new ideas to improve public health.

Unit 11

Track 01

From Seed to T-shirt

T-shirts are a basic part of almost everyone's closet. Over two billion T-shirts are sold every year around the world. So how are they made? And where do they end up?

The story starts with the seed of the cotton plant. The plants are grown on large farms. The cotton is collected and sent to a factory. There, it is cleaned and made into yarn. The yarn is made into cloth. This is used to make T-shirts.

The T-shirts are then transported around the world. Just take a look at the label on one of your T-shirts and see how far it came! The T-shirts go into stores and are sold to consumers. That's you. You probably have the T-shirt for a while, and it is worn, washed, and dried again and again. When you decide to get rid of it, you have a few options. You might throw it in the trash. But if you knew how much of the Earth's natural resources go into making a T-shirt, you might think again! A lot of energy and water are used in making and washing clothes. A lot of chemicals are used in this process, too.

One option is to recycle your old T-shirts. When a T-shirt is sent to a recycling center, it is made into other things, such as cleaning cloths. Another idea is to upcycle your T-shirts. Old T-shirts are sometimes made into belts, scarves, or bags.

Track 02

castle, whistle, wrestle, fasten, listen, soften

Track 03

1 Listen to the way he whistles.
2 You fasten and unfasten the jacket with a zipper.
3 Chemicals are used to soften the cloth.

Track 04

Ryan: My next guest is Angela Miller, and she's here today to talk to us about lucky discoveries. Welcome, Angela. What lucky discovery are you going to tell us about?
Angela: I'm here today to tell you about this material, Ryan.
Ryan: I know that sound. It's Velcro.
Angela: That's right. And did you know that Velcro was invented by a dog?
Ryan: By a dog?!
Angela: Well, almost. Swiss engineer George de Mestral was out with his dog in 1941, and he noticed that some plants stuck to his dog's fur like glue.
Ryan: I know the kind of plant you mean. They're round and sticky.
Angela: Yes. They're called burrs. De Mestral noticed that his dog was covered in burrs. His pants were also covered in them. When he got home, he looked at the plants under a microscope and saw that they had tiny hooks. The fur, and the material of his pants, had small loops. His dog's fur and his pants were caught by the hooks.
Ryan: How was Velcro created from that idea?
Angela: At the time, clothes were made with buttons and zippers. De Mestral wanted to create a new material so people wouldn't need buttons and zippers. It wasn't easy, and it took some time to develop a commercial product, but, after ten years, Velcro was finally created. In the early days, Velcro was made of cotton, but nylon worked better.
Ryan: What was it used for in those days?
Angela: It was used on clothes and bags. It became popular after it was used in space by NASA in the 1960s. It was used by astronauts to hold things in place.
Ryan: Now you can see sneakers that fasten with Velcro. When did it appear on sneakers?
Angela: It was first used on children's sneakers in the 1980s. It's great for children and disabled people because it's very easy to fasten and unfasten.
Ryan: I guess the lesson is to always keep your eyes open because you never know what you might discover. Angela, thank you for joining us today.

Track 05

In today's lecture, I want to tell you about Thato Kgatlhanye. Thato is a young businesswoman from South Africa. She noticed that many poor schoolchildren in South Africa face some problems. First of all, school is often a long way from home. Each morning and evening, these children have to walk many kilometers to school and back again. It is dangerous because there are a lot of cars and trucks on the roads. Second, their homes often don't have electricity. When they get home, they find it difficult to study in the dark.

Track 06

Thato also realized that South Africa has a problem with plastic bags. A lot of plastic bags are thrown away and end up as trash in the streets. In fact, children often carry their books to school in simple plastic bags. Thato thought that she could solve both of these problems. She decided to create schoolbags from recycled plastic bags. They are called Repurpose Schoolbags.

Repurpose Schoolbags were designed to help schoolchildren. They have a solar panel, a battery, and a light. The battery is charged during the day and it powers the light at night. That means that children can do their homework after the sun goes down. They no longer have to hurry home. The bags are also reflective. That means drivers can see the children as they walk along the busy roads. The children are safer. Thato is just one of the many young inventors trying to make life better in Africa.

Track 07

Upcycling Projects

We humans use a lot of materials. Take plastic, for example.

According to Statista, every year, around 350 million metric tons of plastic are produced around the world. Sadly, not much of it is recycled. In fact, about half of the plastic is used just once and is then sent to a landfill, according to Plastic Oceans International. In 2007, Charles Fishman of *Fast Company Magazine* reported that a million plastic bottles are bought every minute of every day in the US, but only around 23% are recycled. Four trillion plastic bags are produced each year, and only 1% are recycled, according to Waste Management. Our use of other plastics is not much better. Plastic use is a big problem.

Many people are looking at ways to upcycle different materials. Upcycling involves finding new uses for materials at the end of their original use. In one project, a greenhouse was created using old plastic water bottles. In others, large coffee cans or old rubber boots were turned into containers for plants, and old rubber tires became notebook covers. Artists, too, upcycle materials. Tim Noble and Sue Webster, two British artists, create what look like piles of trash. When a light shines on the trash from a certain angle, it makes an interesting shadow on the wall.

These days institutions such as colleges and companies are looking for smarter ways to use materials. This involves reducing the amount of materials they use and thinking of ways to upcycle materials so that they last a long time.

Unit 12

Track 01

Types of Community

We all belong to different social groups. We choose some of them ourselves, and some of them are chosen for us. The social groups we belong to often give us support. They also say a lot about who we are and how we see ourselves.

There are many different types of community. One type is community of place. The place could be a neighborhood, a region, or a country. A second is community of interest. The people might all be interested in a certain hobby or a certain type of music, for example. A third is community of purpose. People in this type of community share the same purpose, such as learning a language or running a successful company. A fourth is community of practice. This is a group of people who share the same profession.

Each type of community can offer different things to its members. A community of place might offer people to chat with and to support you in difficult times. A community of interest can give you friendship and a way to learn more about a subject. A community of purpose can help you learn ways of achieving your goals. Also, people working together can often achieve more than a person working by himself or herself. A community of practice gives you opportunities to share ideas as well as the chance to network.

Any particular group might be more than one type of community. For example, a local cycling club is a community of place and a community of interest. If the members decided to raise money for a local charity, they would also be a community of purpose.

Track 02

1	self	**3**	herself	**5**	show
2	your shelf	**4**	sock	**6**	shine

Track 03

Host: Welcome to the show. Today I'm talking to Sean Johnson. Sean's the head of an employment agency and he's going to talk to us about networking. Sean, what is networking?

Sean: Networking is speaking to people in your profession. This gives you a community of practice.

Host: Tell us where we can network and how.

Sean: If you're working, you can start with your office. Try to make time to speak to everyone. If there's someone you haven't met, introduce yourself. Get to know each person. Ask about his or her job. You'll be surprised how much you can learn just from chatting with people.

Host: What if you don't have a job yet?

Sean: You can start to find contacts in your chosen profession. Start with friends and family. Maybe you already know someone who works in an area you are interested in. Think about people you knew in college. What are they doing now? Maybe they can help you when you are job hunting. That's a good example of why you should always stay in touch with people from high school when you go to college, or with old colleagues when you start a new job.

Host: What about online groups?

Sean: They can be a great way of sharing ideas. Find a group connected to the profession you want. Ask questions, join discussions, and comment on posts. You'll learn about your profession and get to know people. You might even hear about job opportunities before other people do.

Host: Does all networking happen online?

Sean: Not at all. Your college might organize a career fair when companies come to campus. That's a good chance to speak to people in your future profession. You can also contact companies directly and ask about opportunities to work as an intern. You don't always get paid, but you get a lot of experience. Another interesting option is speed networking. Some colleges and companies organize these events. You have a few minutes to talk to one person, then everyone changes partners. That way, you can make a lot of useful connections in a very short time.

Host: Thanks, Sean. So what do you think about networking? Call us now and tell us.

Track 04

Hello and welcome to today's podcast. I want to talk to you today about different social groups. You might see people who wear dark clothes, dark make-up, and call themselves *goths*. Others, such as *otakus*, might dress as characters from comics or video games. We call these youth subcultures, or youth tribes. They often have one thing in common. You can see who is a part of the group by looking at them. They dress differently from other young people. There are three reasons for this.

First, many young people want to look different from their parents to show that they are a new generation. This has been true for decades. American teenagers in the 1940s started to wear jeans and T-shirts when their parents often wore shirts and ties. It was a way of saying: "We're here, and we're different."

At the same time, young people want to feel like part of a group. They want to spend time with other young people who share their opinions and beliefs. When you are part of a youth tribe, you can see who is like you and who is different, even if you've never met them before. If they are in the same youth tribe, they probably have the same interests as you.

Finally, young people want to express their personality. They choose a sub-culture that shows who they are. And, of course, that can change. Today's goth might be tomorrow's hipster. So, what do you think of youth subcultures? Contact me and I'll read some of your comments on the next podcast.

Track 05

Reaching a Target Group

Sometimes, a business has a product that it wants to sell to a certain group of people. For example, there is no point advertising a new car to people who don't drive. Governments, too, sometimes want to get information to a specific group. This might be information about children's health that they want to give to parents. In both cases, it would be a waste of money to inform everyone. It's better to aim your message at the people you want to reach. How do you do that?

First of all, it's important to clearly identify the group of people you want to reach. Is it parents? Is it teenagers? Is it homeowners? When you have a clear idea of your target group, then you can think about how to reach people in the group.

Second, you need to think about how to communicate with that group. Teenagers and young adults spend time on social networks. That might be the best way to reach them. It might not work so well for senior citizens or other groups.

Third, you need to express your message in the right way. With professional people, you may want to use serious language. With teenagers, you may want to use slang or informal language.

When you aim your message at a clear target group and use the right form of communication, your message is more effective.

Macmillan Education
4 Crinan Street
London N1 9XW
A division of Macmillan Education Limited

Companies and representatives throughout the world

Speak Your Mind Level 2B Student's Book
ISBN 978-1-380-03126-6
Speak Your Mind Level 2B Student's Book + access to Student's App and access to Digital Workbook
ISBN 978-1-380-03859-3
Speak Your Mind Level 2B Student's Book + access to Student's App ISBN 978-1-380-03860-9

Written by Mickey Rogers, Joanne Taylore-Knowles, and Steve Taylore-Knowles

First published 2020

Designed by QBS Learning
Illustrated by Keith Favazza (Wendy Lynn & Co.) pp. 88, 102; QBS Learning pp. 92, 109.
Cover design by therestless.co.uk
Cover photographs by Getty Images/Chatuporn Sornlampoo/EyeEm (background); Shutterstock/leungchopan (lower body), Shutterstock/Dima Sidelnikov (upper body), Shutterstock/ventdusud (window).
Picture research by Fernanda Rocha/Ikonia LLC

Authors' acknowledgements
Mickey, Jo, and Steve would like to thank everyone at Macmillan Education and RedNova Learning who have made this project possible and who have gone the extra mile (literally!) to meet up, work together, and throw around a million ideas, some of which even made their way into the books! Jo and Steve would also like to thank Scout for her patience and understanding and for letting her parents get on with it when they needed to!

The publishers would like to thank all the teachers that piloted and reviewed the series, and a special thanks to Annette Flavel for content and cultural reviews.

The authors and publishers would like to thank the following for permission to reproduce their photographs:
Alamy Stock Photo/Andor Bujdoso pp. 86, 134, Alamy Stock Photo/Hero Images Inc. p. 113, Alamy Stock Photo/Carolyn Jenkins p. 114(t), Alamy Stock Photo/Jochen Tack p. 90, Alamy Stock Photo/Tetra Images, LLC pp. 92(3), 93; **Getty Images**/ajr_images p. 83, Getty Images/Luis Alvarez pp. 126, 138, Getty Images/Yuri Arcurs p. 85, Getty Images/Aurora Open/Steve Glass p. 102(br), Getty Images/Paul Bradbury p. 100(7), Getty Images/Adie Bush p. 77, Getty Images/Jasper Cole p. 78(4), Getty Images/Dziggyfoto p. 78(2), Getty Images/Hero Images 80(cl), Getty Images/iStockphoto/monkeybusinessimages p. 80(bl), Getty Images/Johner Images p. 94, Getty Images/Jupiterimages p. 111, Getty Images/Thomas Northcut p. 110(tr), Getty Images/NoSystem images p. 84, Getty Images/HUGO PHILPOTT/Staff p. 114(b), Getty Images/Serghei Starus/EyeEm p. 92(5), Getty Images/Westend61 p. 80(tl), **Science Photo Library**/TEK IMAGE pp. 106, 136; **Shutterstock**/Africa Studio pp. 92(4), 105(tl), Shutterstock/ajt p. 115, Shutterstock/aklionka p. 124, Shutterstock/AnastasiaKopa p. 100(3), Shutterstock/ArtFamily p. 82(br), Shutterstock/ArtOfPhotos p. 77, Shutterstock/ESB Professional p. 125(1), Shutterstock/Evgeny Atamanenko p. 92(7), Shutterstock/beeboys p. 91, Shutterstock/Beer5020 p. 67, Shutterstock/bellena p. 110(bl), Shutterstock/Diego Cervo p. 100(8), Shutterstock/chainarong06 p. 105(tm), Shutterstock/CHAjAMP p. 100(6), Shutterstock/Tasha Cherkasova p. 74(t), Shutterstock/Chinnapong p. 97, Shutterstock/dnd_project pp. 96, 135, Shutterstock/Vikentiy Elizarov p. 107, Shutterstock/ESB Professional p. 72, Shuttestock/Anna Gorodnitskaya p. 122(1), Shutterstock/gpointstudio p. 125(3), Shutterstock/g-stockstudio p. 122(2), Shutterstock/JM Travel Photography p. 70, Shutterstock/Kamira p. 110(tm), Shutterstock/Kingcraft p. 110(br), Shutterstock/Olesya Kuznetsova p. 78(3), Shutterstock/Soloviova Liudmyla p. 117, Shutterstock/LukaKikina p. 110(bm), Shutterstock/Muskoka Stock Photos p. 120(br), Shutterstock/Nattakorn_Maneerat p. 100(2), Shutterstock/Maridav p. 100(4), Shutterstock/Natalia Mels p. 104, Shutterstock/Monkey Business Images p. 99, Shutterstock/Monster Ztudio pp. 116, 137, Shutterstock/tanya_morozz pp. 104-105(b), Shutterstock/Mr.anaked p. 112(b), Shutterstock/MyImages - Micha p. 92(2), Shutterstock/NATNN p. 109, Shuttestock/OPOLJA p. 120, Shutterstock/P A p. 122(3), Shutterstock/panotthorn phuhual p. 110(tl), Shutterstock/Igor Plotnikov p. 87, Shutterstock/Dmitrii Pridannikov p. 92(1), Shutterstock/raksapon p. 110(br), Shutterstock/Rawpixel.com pp. 118, 141, Shutterstock/Huguette Roe p. 112(t), Shutterstock/ShotPrime Studio p. 108, Shutterstock/sirtravelalot p. 100(1), Shutterstock/Oleksii Stebliuk p. 123, Shutterstock/StockLite p. 105(tr), Shutterstock/Mila Supinskaya Glashchenko p. 82(tr), Shutterstock/Syda Productions p. 125(2), Shutterstock/Viktoriya p. 98, Shutterstock/vipman p. 92(6), Shutterstock/Tom Wang p. 68, Shutterstock/wavebreakmedia p. 125(4), Shutterstock/yurakrasil p. 78(1), Shutterstock/88studio p. 74(bl); **123RF**/Monchai Tudsamalee p. 100(5).

Additional Sources:
p. 76, *State of Create Study* by Adobe, 2012, Adobe website. p. 76, CEO Study by IBM, 2010, IBM website. p. 76, *Wired to Create: Unraveling the Mysteries of the Creative Mind* by Scott Barry Kaufman and Carolyn Grego, 2015 (cited in "7 Surprising Facts About Creativity, According to Science," by John Paul Titlow, September 16, 2016, *Fast Company*. p. 82, "Five Reasons Why We Should All Learn How to Do Nothing," by Oliver Burkeman, January 9, 2015, *The Guardian*. p. 98, "10 Ways to Improve Your Brain Health," by Bryan Roche, July 17, 2014, *Psychology Today*. p. 98, "How to Boost Your Brain," by Hannah Nichols, January 10, 2018, *Medical News Today*. p. 98, "Nine Ways to Make Yourself Smarter," by Joseph Mercola, 2012, Mercola.com. p. 98, "This Is the Only Type of Brain Training that Works, According to Science," by Michael Grothaus, August 21, 2017, *Fast Company*. p. 108, "55 Things You Probably Didn't Know About T-Shirts," by mcc_northcutt, February 15, 2016, The BlueCotton Blog. p. 126, "Entrepreneurship Rankings," 2018, U.S. *News & World Report*.

Printed and bound in Mexico
by Compañía Editorial Ultra, S.A. de C.V.

2021 2020
12 11 10 09